THE TREASURE

IN THE FIELD

Advancing the Kingdom of God

By

Dr John W. McElroy

THE TREASURE IN THE FIELD

Printed in Australia

ISBN: 978-0-6451627-1-4

TABLE OF CONTENTS

FOREWORD

The church today must navigate through numerous perilous currents! The politics and culture of many nations are no longer functioning from a moral or righteous Christian foundation. Many are submitting to the narratives of cultural Marxism, gender fluidity, and various other godless and antichrist systems!

The fruit of these great lies and clever deceptions is: increased crime and corruption, increased drug and alcohol addiction, increased legislation against the covenant of marriage between a man and a woman, the rise of abortion—now more than double the birth rate, a rampant divorce rate, destruction of family identity, and welfare subsidies making it almost impossible to be married and financially provide for the family. The Church is increasingly being attacked by: legislative actions, educational elites and their institutions, and the liberal, leftist, socialist media, and politicians. Most of these embrace an antichrist and antichurch demonic spirit.

To counteract this activity, all Christians and church leaders must make the necessary changes to become truth-seekers and truth-tellers. It's time to draw courage and be strengthened by the Word of God including Psalm 15:1-5.

"LORD, who may abide in Your tabernacle? Who may dwell in Your holy hill? He who walks uprightly, And works righteousness, And speaks the truth in his heart..."

The Bible is full of scriptures that admonish us to change, adapt, form coalitions of like-minded believers, and most of all—stand up and speak out!

John McElroy's wonderful work, *The Treasure in the Field,* is a truth-telling adventure and discovery that can help you through your own changes and to adapt to God's words and ways. This is one of the most honest depictions of trials, struggles, changes, adapting, and overcoming that I have read to date! This book is a must read for anyone involved and those who desire to become involved in Christian ministry.

Remember, the Gospel message never changes—but we must change and keep maturing from "faith to faith" to "glory to glory"! May we all be Holy Spirit-led truth-tellers, founded on the Word of God, who constantly seek and speak God's wisdom and truth!

See you on the battlefield!

Apostle John P. Kelly

Convening Apostle

International Coalition of Apostolic Leaders (ICAL)

Acknowledgments

This book could not have been written without the support of my wife, Alaine, and son, Toby. Alaine stood faithfully by me on the journey. Thank you, Alaine, for proofreading the manuscript and Toby for designing the amazing cover. Maya Krayneva, our talented spiritual daughter, has been invaluable in editing, formatting, and arranging the publication and distribution of the book. I am grateful to Dr John Kelly, my wise spiritual father, for writing the Foreword.

I am dedicating this book to the memory of my dear friend, the late Alwyn Keith Richards. Alwyn was a successful farmer, visionary, church elder, spiritual father, and a Barnabas (son of encouragement) to me. He gave me his valuable time and counsel during the early years of Churchlands. I am grateful to Alwyn's family for contributing toward producing the book.

Much of my story relates to the history of Churchlands Christian Fellowship. I am grateful to the two gifted men who served as Chairmen of the Elders at Churchlands, Hans Van Wijngaarden, and Fred Boshart. Thank you also to the many staff and volunteers on the Churchlands team who played a huge part in fulfilling our vision of a lighthouse and the tree.

I also recognize the love and support of my colleagues at Southern Cross Centre, the Southern Cross Association of Churches, and the National Council of the Australian Coalition of Apostolic Leaders in helping to write this story. I am so grateful God brought you into my life and for inspiring me to write this book.

In recent years, my horizons have been broadened by being part of the International Coalition of Apostolic Leaders. I have stood on the shoulders of spiritual giants like Papa John Kelly, Dr Joseph Mattera, David Balestri, Mark Pfeifer, and Hubie Synn. Thank you.

Introduction

The Great Reset

The Church, as we know it, is about to change. The Body of Christ is being shaken and compelled to re-examine its priorities and practices. No Christian denomination, movement, or group will be exempt from this spiritual tsunami. God, in His mercy, is returning His Church to the priorities and practices of Jesus and the apostles.

2020 will be remembered as the year when the shaking began. As the first pandemic in a century brought the world to its knees, it was apparent that previous realities were poised for a major reset. How we interpret this reset depends on our closeness to God. For the world's 'elites' and 'progressives', this reset points to a humanistic agenda of globalization and establishing a new world order. Citizens of God's Kingdom see it differently. God is turning up the heat to break the religious spirit and return His Church to New Testament foundations.

Governments were caught off guard by the Covid-19 pandemic. Within weeks, entire nations went into lockdown to contain the pandemic. With gatherings prohibited and social distancing enforced, citizens in every nation faced unprecedented challenges. Churches were not exempt. Sunday services were suspended or severely restricted and many had to close their doors.

Freedom Under Threat

In addition to freedom of assembly, freedom of speech and religion would come under threat. In 2020, the Government of the Australian State of Victoria announced it would introduce 'conversion suppression' legislation. This bill made it a criminal offense for any person, including pastors, counsellors or medical practitioners, to influence anyone experiencing sexual disorientation or gender dysphoria.

While the rationale behind this law was to curb what are perceived as cruel or forced therapies on those with same sex attraction or gender dysphoria, the legislation goes further. It decrees severe punishment for interfering with the normalization of homosexual or transgender preferences. Conservative Australian Christians are about to face, for the first time, criminal charges and severe penalties for obeying what they believe the Bible teaches regarding sexuality and gender.

Early in 2021, the Victorian legislation was passed by a bipartisan majority in the State Parliament. Having the Victorian stamp of approval, state governments across Australia are poised to introduce similar legislation. Christians holding Biblical views on marriage, sexuality, and gender, must not ignore the threat to their religious freedom and freedom of speech.

Discovering God's Kingdom

The time has come to ask: How have we come to this point? Why are nations founded on Judeo-Christian principles now legislating for lifestyles that are contrary to Biblical teaching? The answer points to the current state of the Church. For decades, rather than engage the world, churches often focused on how to escape it. By failing to engage society and establish the Kingdom of God on the earth, atheistic and humanistic ideologies now fill the gap. When Christian voices are silent, the world descends into moral confusion, lawlessness, and division.

Jesus gave His disciples a mandate to be the light of the world and the salt of the earth. The Church was not meant to be sidelined or intimidated into silence. In Acts 4, Peter and John were commanded by the Jewish Sanhedrin to stop speaking about Jesus. Their response was a bold rebuttal of their critics, "We must obey God rather than men". They feared nothing and refused to stop speaking about Jesus.

The title of this book, *The Treasure in the Field*, comes from Jesus' Parable in Matthew 13:44, "The kingdom of heaven is like a treasure hidden in a field. When a man found it, he hid it again, and then in joy went and sold all he had and bought that field."

The treasure of God's Kingdom is still hidden to many in the Church. In search of God's treasure, I have surveyed many fields and knocked on many doors. I read books, listened to speakers, and served in the houses of several masters in search for authentic Christianity. I knew Jesus' message was the Gospel of the Kingdom but discovered that few Christian leaders appreciate its significance.

Reset is Reformation

Churches fail to be the salt and light when their leaders fail to see the world through a Kingdom of God lens. Without a Kingdom perspective, God's people revert to lesser priorities. God is shaking the Church to get our attention and re-focus our priorities. Churches need more than another revival, they need reformation. Reformation comes when God's people return to scriptural truths that are forgotten.

Reformation does not happen overnight, it comes through a process of *recognition, realignment,* and *revolution.* Change begins with the *recognition* of a problem. The Church in its current form is losing the battle against the kingdom of darkness. *Recognition* brings *realignment. Realignment* comes when we employ the priorities and practices of Jesus and the apostles that are relevant today. *Revolution* comes when the Kingdom of God begins to permeate the foundations of society.

Structure of the Book

This book is divided into three parts:

♔ Part I: The Birth of a Vision.

I will recount how God birthed a vision in me for the future of His Church. My journey with God spans over four decades. I will highlight experiences in ministry, in denominations, movements, and networks. This provides a context for my conclusions about the current state of the Church.

♛ Part II: The Journey

On my ministry journey, the Lord continued to shape my perspectives through a series of diverse experiences. Gradually, I came to see that God was configuring me to pioneer a new wineskin for the Church. The lessons I learned in this phase would someday guide in establishing a church on New Testament foundations.

♛ Part III: The Prototype.

Finally, we examine the components of a Kingdom configured Church. Jesus' priority was the Gospel of the Kingdom of God. The apostles' priorities are seen in the life of three New Testament churches and Paul's missionary journeys. Our goal must be to develop prototypes and working models of a new church wineskin. We examine the blueprint of a work in progress, Southern Cross Centre.

Jesus called His Church to be the light of the world and the salt of the earth. This means we must work with God to establish His Kingdom on earth. The time has come. The Kingdom of God is near. Repent and believe the Good News!

The time has come.
The Kingdom of God is near.
Repent and believe the good news!

MARK 1:15

Part One: Birth
of a Vision

CHAPTER ONE: THE JOURNEY BEGINS

Without faith it is impossible to please God because
anyone who comes to Him must believe that He exists
and that He rewards those who earnestly seek Him.

HEBREWS 11:6

*Like many people in the Bible, my journey with God began when He
revealed Himself in a vision. After this, new and challenging opportunities
began to open up to me. As I faced my fears and said yes to new
challenges, I began to grow. There is always an element of risk in faith.
Whether we get things right or wrong, nothing God initiates goes to
waste. In every situation God imparts important lessons that will assist
us in the future.*

To reach the port of heaven we
must sail, sometimes with the
wind and sometimes against
it—but we must sail, not drift or
lie at anchor.

OLIVER WENDEL HOLMES

Trains and Sunsets

My journey with God began in a railway town in the Midwestern state of Iowa. Some of my fondest memories trace back to train journeys I took with my father. Dad grew up on a farm during the Great Depression. The main line of the Burlington Northern Railway passed along the farm's northern boundary. My father often talked about the day in 1934 when he and his dad watched the first dawn to dusk passenger train pass on its journey from Chicago to Denver.

Passenger trains were still a popular mode of travel in America in the 1960s. When I was ten years old, Dad took me on my first train trip to Chicago. Although the journey was only six hours, it seemed longer because of the many stops on the way. I felt so grown up looking out the window of the gleaming stainless-steel carriage that took us toward the 'windy city'.

I inherited my dad's love of trains. One of my most memorable Christmases was when Santa brought me a model train set. The set was only a miniature version of what I heard day and night when growing up. I was fascinated by the blaring whistles, whirring diesel engines, and crash of boxcars as they connected to long freight trains.

Dad and I would often take long walks at sunset to the train station. The California Zephyr stopped every evening at our local station on its westward journey to San Francisco. After ten minutes at the platform, the conductor yelled, "All aboard!" His words brought the train to life! A sharp foghorn whistle blew, the engines whirred, and bells began to clang. Slowly the magnificent Zephyr gathered speed. Soon, all that remained was a red dot on the horizon atop the gleaming rails.

Spirit of Adventure

Something was birthed in me as I watched those trains. I think it was a spirit of adventure. I longed to be on the Zephyr, speeding west toward destinations that were over the horizon. Little did I realize was that someday travel would be a large part of my life.

Progressing from childhood into my teens, I was only twelve when my mother bought me my first guitar, a cheap $10 model with steel strings that cut deep into my fingers. Music would open some amazing doors later in my life.

I enjoyed my early school years. In junior high, I became involved in our church's youth group. Our pastors were great with young people. They talked a lot about the need for personal faith in Christ. I came to see the Christian life as very attractive. Being part of the youth group, my first experiences of ministry were through music and public speaking. Even though I did not know much about God, I always felt close to Him and believed He had a purpose for my life.

By the time I graduated from high school, I was elected as vice-president of the student council, became an Eagle Scout, sang and acted in many drama productions, and was appointed as a youth representative to the Iowa Crime Commission. Each experience helped me grow in confidence and how to relate to people.

Following high school, I was not sure which university to enrol in. Choosing a safe and economical option, I signed up for a two-year degree at a local college. I wanted to study pre-law. I chose law, thinking it might lead to a career in politics. I wanted to see the world become a better place. Politics seemed a good place to begin.

A Life-changing Encounter

After making a re-commitment to Christ, I felt drawn to a coffeehouse that served as a drop-in centre for youth in our city. The coffeehouse was a place where I could learn more about God and the Bible. One autumn evening, I met a friend there to pray and seek direction for my life.

While praying, something unexpected happened. With eyes closed, I saw a figure standing in front of me. I never had a vision before. At first the figure was fuzzy, but gradually I saw the outline of a man dressed in white. As he moved closer, I noticed him wearing a robe and sandals. He carried a shepherd's crook.

Looking at his face was like looking into the sun. I could see the man's left hand extended toward me, holding a shepherd's crook. He spoke, not with a natural voice, but kind of telepathically, *This is what you will be in my hands*. Then he disappeared.

After some time, I opened my eyes. My companion was still sitting nearby. I thought for a second, *Did this really happen?* Then I blurted out, "I think I just saw Jesus!" At the time, I had no idea of how this encounter would shape my future.

Spiritual Parents

After that night, I began dropping into the coffeehouse almost every weekend. I was soon invited to a Wednesday night study group led by a couple named Don and Pat.

Don and Pat held positions at a local vocational training college and were excellent teachers. The group studied three books: *The Vision* by David Wilkerson, *The Holy Spirit and You* by Dennis and Rita Bennett, and *The Late Great Planet Earth* by Hal Lindsay. These amazing books sparked my interest in prophecy, the gifts of the Holy Spirit, and eschatology.

Gradually, Don and Pat became a spiritual father and mother to me. They said I had the capacity to understand God's Word. I felt honored that they would spend time mentoring me. Unfortunately, our connection, at least in Iowa, was short-lived. They left their education careers to pastor a growing church called Life Unlimited in Odessa, Texas.

We remained in contact and they invited me to visit and preach at one of their services. Immediately, I started saving for the trip. The Lord provided and within months I found myself preaching at their evening service. I will never forget that night! I was nervous and felt like my heart was stuck in my throat. When I finished, a very stately looking man approached me. He said, "Son, I prophesy that someday you will be the pastor of a very large church." Was this a confirmation that God was calling me into ministry?

Open Doors and God's Provision

Jesus taught that before building a tower, we should always count the cost. Having grown up in a Presbyterian church, I knew that to become a pastor required years of study. Doing further research, I discovered that ordination, at least in the Presbyterian Church, required both a bachelor's and master's degree.

After much prayer and discussing the matter with my mom and dad, I applied to attend the University of Dubuque and its graduate school, Dubuque Theological Seminary. Doors then began to open. My application was accepted.

Next, I heard of a grant from an educational trust open only to students studying for the ministry in Iowa. I was petrified when I drove to the capital city of Des Moines and was interviewed by a group of lawyers. The Lord gave me incredible favor. I received a grant that paid for my books and study resources for the next four years!

Many students have to borrow money to finance their tertiary education. This leaves debts that must be paid off after graduation. Miraculously, the University of Dubuque offered me a scholarship to pay all my tuition for the first year. Then, the elders of my home church, at the urging of my Pastor, agreed to pay my tuition costs for the remaining 3 years at Dubuque Seminary.

The Lord provided for my living costs through a weekend student pastoral position at a Presbyterian church in a small country town near my parents. For three and a half years, Tuesday to Friday, I studied at the university and seminary. I would then drive 220 kilometres to work from Saturday to Monday.

The people in the church were fantastic! I was only twenty-one, had no experience in ministry, and was totally dependent on God's provision. Over the next three years I fell in love with the people in that rural community.

Alaine

Nearing the end of my Seminary studies, I began to consider my next stage of life and what God had in store. I would soon reconnect with Alaine, a girl I met in my hometown as a Rotary exchange student

Alaine was from Perth, Western Australia. Perth is the only Australian capital city situated on the Indian Ocean. It is a beautiful and modern city, with spacious parks, lakes, and beaches. Perth is known as the most isolated capital city in the world with a population of over two million. When I first met Alaine it was half that size.

Alaine and I met at a choir rehearsal at the Presbyterian Church in the middle of winter. She came to Iowa as a Rotary exchange student to repeat her final year of high school. Alaine was unprepared for the bitterly cold temperatures. The night we met was snowy and freezing, I offered Alaine a ride home from rehearsal and was encouraged when she accepted.

Alaine and I became friends and went out socially for about six months. Romance was not on our minds at that point. By the end of the year, Alaine had made many friends. I was part of a large crowd who farewelled her at the airport when she returned to Perth. For two years we went our separate ways with only an occasional letter.

I remember a friend telling me that Alaine was returning to Iowa at Christmas and that she was looking forward to seeing me. This perked my interest. By then, I was halfway through Seminary and pastoring on weekends. Seeing Alaine at the Christmas party, she seemed more relaxed and had become a charming, attractive young woman. We had a great conversation and I invited her to sing at my church at a Sunday service. She accepted.

Getting Married

About a year later, nearing the end of my studies, I began to consider marriage. For nearly four years I had been in a long-distance relationship, but things just did not seem right. In desperation, I drove to a park and, at the top of a hill, prayed that God would guide me to the right woman.

Exactly a week later, I received an aerogramme (airmail letter) from Alaine. With uncharacteristic boldness, she asked if I thought there could ever be a future between us?

After discussing the matter with my parents, I phoned Alaine, "There's only one way to find out. Can I come visit you in Perth?" Within four months, we were engaged. Three months later my family and I travelled to Perth for the wedding.

Return to Iowa

Two weeks later we all returned to Iowa. With one semester of Seminary left, Alaine and I began our married lives together in that small country town.

For nearly four years we lived happily in Sigourney, Iowa. I was ordained in 1978 and continued as the pastor of a small Presbyterian church. Alaine directed the choir.

In 1979, I enrolled in a Doctor of Ministry program at San Francisco Theological Seminary. As part of the course, I was required to spend a summer in residence at the Seminary. As Alaine and I drove home to Iowa, we sensed change was coming.

Adventure Across the Vast Pacific

A pastoral position had recently opened up in a Uniting Church in Perth. I was invited to apply, but it would require a five-year commitment. Thinking this was a long time to be overseas, I declined the offer.

After several months, I felt no peace, so I inquired if the position was still open. It was. We accepted a call into the All Saints Uniting Church in Floreat Park, Western Australia.

Moving to Australia was a huge decision, but we sensed it was the right one. Miraculously, my Australian permanent residency visa was approved quickly. In May 1981, after many tearful goodbyes, we began a new adventure across the vast Pacific.

When I received God's shepherd's crook, He launched a series of events that were beyond my comprehension. I had no idea how moving to Australia would change the course of my life.

Lessons Learned   The Journey Begins

MARRIAGE

Next to the decision to follow Jesus, who we marry is our most important decision in life. I did not know Alaine well when we married, nor she me, yet we made the right decision. Marrying the right person accelerated my pathway into God's purposes.

PREPARATION

God opened doors to prepare me for leadership long before I became a pastor. My experiences in school, boy scouts, and numerous leadership roles shaped in me confidence and skills I would require later in life.

SPIRITUAL PARENTS

Embracing a spiritual father and mother, Don and Pat, accelerated my growth. They highlighted what they saw in me that confirmed God's call on my life. We learn how to become a spiritual father or mother by first becoming a spiritual son or daughter.

WISE COUNSEL

God opened doors but I had to take initiative and act on opportunities as they presented. We should always seek wise counsel. Proverbs 15:22, "Plans fail for lack of counsel, but with many advisers they succeed."

EDUCATION

A good education is an asset for life. I am grateful to have had a good education. Even though the course was strict and demanding, I am grateful for the Biblical, leadership, and pastoral perspectives I now have as a result.

PEOPLE

God intends for us to have three kinds of people in our lives:

1) a Paul figure—someone who we may not meet with frequently but who we look up to and whose model we want to observe.

2) a Barnabas—a spiritual mother or father who speaks into our lives and we can interact with regularly.

3) a Timothy—a younger or less mature son or daughter who we are building into.

SMALL BEGINNINGS

Never despise the day of small beginnings. I was blessed to have started in ministry in a small, rural community. If we are faithful in small things, God will eventually increase our responsibilities and sphere of influence.

CHAPTER TWO: MOVING TO AUSTRALIA

By faith Abraham, when called to go to a place he would later receive as his inheritance, obeyed and went, even though he did not know where he was going.

HEBREWS 11:8

Four years after Alaine and I were married, we accepted God's call to leave Iowa and pastor a church in Perth, Western Australia. We knew little about the church and the denomination we had been called to. God opens doors that can take us well outside of our comfort zone. During our five years at All Saints Floreat, the church grew numerically and spiritually. This rapid growth, however, set the stage for a bitter church split. Through the split, God set in motion events that would take us in a new and unexpected direction.

The greatest pleasure I know is to do a good action by stealth and to have found out by accident.

CHARLES LAMB

Culture Shock

Landing at Perth Airport gave Alaine and me a sense of déjà vu. Exactly four years earlier, Alaine was waiting to introduce me to her family and friends. Now, Alaine's family were gathered to welcome us to a new home and new responsibilities.

The magnitude of our decision was beginning to hit me. I had made a five-year commitment to pastor a group of people I had never met. I knew even less about the Uniting Church.

Most Americans have a very romanticized view of Australia. Hollywood blockbuster movies, like *The Man from Snowy River* and *Crocodile Dundee*, paint a picture of the land down-under as the last frontier. While this is partially true, it is also the land of the 'long weekend', stunning beaches, modern cities, and unusual plants and animals. My first task was to get to know the *real* Australia.

Australians and Americans share a common language, but that is where most similarities end. Australia has an intriguing culture, a rich history, and a fascinating way of mixing formality and informality. While most Aussies enjoy their weekends relaxing at the beach or taking short trips to the country, life is very different for a pastor. Sundays are a time to shepherd the faithful minority of Aussies who are involved in a local church.

Having been raised in the American Midwest, where church attendance was common, I was shocked to discover that only about one in ten Australians attend Sunday worship services. This troubled me. How could a nation be so apparently indifferent to God? Why was the Church so marginalized? Could anything be done to reverse this state of affairs?

Diversity at All Saints Floreat

In May 1981, I was installed as a minister of the word in the Uniting Church (UCA). The denomination was only four years old when I arrived. The UCA was formed in 1977 by a merger of the Methodist, Presbyterian, and Congregational churches across Australia.

I was curious about why the three denominations merged. Some said it was to fulfil Jesus' prayer for unity in John 17:21, "that all of them (who believe in Him) may be one." Others argued that the three denominations were losing members at an alarming rate.

All Saints Floreat was seen as a desirable placement in the Uniting Church. Floreat Park is known as Perth's garden suburb. It is located near the coast, has many lovely parks, and impressive residences with well-manicured gardens.

The church building boasted a modern and picturesque sanctuary. Its modern design made it a popular wedding venue. Many of the church's members were affluent professionals or businesspeople. Following our arrival, we were invited to many dinner parties and social events.

The church was surprisingly diverse, both culturally and theologically. About half the congregation were Australians and the remainder hailed from a plethora of nations. My expository preaching soon brought a response from those of a more liberal persuasion. I sensed a need to strengthen the congregation's knowledge of God's Word and to introduce the ministry of the Holy Spirit.

New Programs

My predecessor had been a senior man who had a reputation as an excellent preacher. I felt the same was expected of me. He had left All Saints at short notice to accept a call to a congregation near Melbourne. This left some members with unresolved grief. While this was concerning, there was little I could do to bring their old pastor back.

To get better acquainted, Alaine and I hosted a series of manse (pastor's house) nights. During our first year, we regularly invited members of the church into our home for supper (evening tea and desserts). From these evenings, we gradually got to know people. I was intrigued to get to know people from such diverse cultural backgrounds.

It did not take long until we were caught up in a flurry of activity. We began with a men's weekday Bible study group. Then, to strengthen Biblical foundations, we introduced the Bethel Bible Series. Over the next two-years, I trained twenty men and women to teach Bethel. The series was a great success, except to the liberals, who criticized it as being too 'fundamentalist'.

Alaine directed the church choir each Sunday morning. In the afternoons, we started a youth group called Lightshine. With a talented team of singers and dancers, we put together a Christian rock musical to perform at churches and schools around WA. The Lightshine Group grew to nearly a hundred high school and college kids. It was attractive because it included a blend of music, testimonies, and Bible study in an informal setting. Many kids grew closer to God in the group.

Church Growth

All Saints started to grow as new families were attracted to the church. The children's ministry soon outgrew the existing church hall. Instead of building a new education wing onto the church, we decided to use the manse next door for children's ministry.

When nearby residents got wind of our plans to transform the manse, they circulated a petition to oppose our expansion. While the neighbors were unsuccessful, their opposition revealed their resentment toward having a church in their residential area.

Alaine and I had to find alternative accommodation. When asked if we'd like to buy or rent a home nearby, we chose to build a new home in the nearby subdivision of Floreat Waters. As we did not have sufficient savings for a house loan deposit, members of All Saints and nearby churches established a fund to loan us the shortfall. We were very grateful!

Personal Growth

During these first years in Australia, I spent many nights writing my dissertation for a Doctor of Ministry Degree at San Francisco Theological Seminary. My topic was: *A Study of the Identity and Mission of the Uniting Church in Western Australia*. I chose this topic for two reasons: it would enhance my perspective on ministry in Australia and provide a valuable resource to assist Uniting Church members understand the new denomination and how it came to be.

For five years, I saturated myself in the denomination's history, theology, and mission. I interviewed dozens of church members all over the state. My research and interviews were enlightening. They gave me a deeper understanding, not only of the UCA, but of the reasons why many Australians resisted attending church.

When the dissertation was complete, my findings were presented in a study booklet. When I inquired about financial help to print it, the response was disappointing. Unfortunately, the study booklet never went to print.

Rumblings of Discontent

Blissfully unaware of any problems, Alaine and I travelled to San Francisco to attend the graduation ceremony. Completing the thesis had been a major goal for me. I travelled to the US with the satisfaction that I had written something of great value for the UCA. At my graduation ceremony, Alaine was pregnant with our first child. I saw this as a double blessing.

Following our return from the US, we became aware that there were some rumblings of discontent at All Saints. Alaine was by now in the latter stage of her pregnancy. Some long-time members no longer felt comfortable in their church. The influx of new people had been unsettling. They no longer felt a sense of connection.

We were also told that some members were unhappy that Alaine and I were planning to build our own home. A rumor was circulating that we were building a mansion! The minister had always lived in the manse. Finally, there were murmurs I had used time from when I was paid by the church to write my Doctoral thesis.

John Wimber Conference

Soon after our return from San Francisco, my good friend, Alwyn Richards, offered to pay my way to attend a John Wimber conference in Auckland, New Zealand. I had heard about Wimber and his unusual gift of moving in the power of the Holy Spirit.

The conference in Auckland was life changing! The Bible came to life as I saw, for the first time, New Testament signs and wonders. I resolved to invite John Wimber to Perth.

The flight home from Auckland was delayed for two days as a result of aircraft problems. Eventually, at 3:15 AM on a Sunday morning I arrived back in Perth.

On Trial

Totally exhausted, I was met at Perth Airport by one the church elders. I will never forget his words, "Things are not good. You need to be at the church service this morning!"

I discovered that a formal complaint had been made to the Perth Presbytery accusing me of not being a pastor to the "entire" congregation, but only those who embraced my views. I was shocked.

What transpired over the next three months was very sad. I later discovered that four out of the fifteen All Saints Elders had asked the Presbytery to intervene and bring me into line with congregational expectations. Their strategy was that I would either comply or be replaced. I was told that a congregational meeting had been scheduled so people could air their grievances.

As the meeting began, one prominent member stood and presented a list of over twenty accusations against me. As they were read out, one by one, there were cheers of agreement. I was shocked when I realized, I was on trial. The chairman struggled to regain control of the meeting. I wondered, *Are these the same people I thought were my friends?*

Following the meeting, the congregation appeared evenly split, for and against me. I had been naïve, unaware of the impact that rapid change would have in this rather conservative and established congregation. I have also come to see that, at times, I lacked maturity in my leadership. I was unwise by trying to change the status quo too quickly.

Stand and See Your Deliverance

Once the dust settled, I asked, *Lord, what are you saying, and what shall we do?*

Within days, I received a prophetic word that I will never forget. "If you leave the scene of your trials, what you fear most will follow you and consume you. But if you stand in obedience to my Word, in due time, I will lift you up and place you in the land where you belong. Stand and see my deliverance."

So, what happened then? Those who remained at All Saints eventually merged with the nearby Forum Uniting Church. The All Saints building was torn down and the surrounding land subdivided into three residential blocks. Proceeds from the sale were used to build a new worship centre on the Forum property. The new church was renamed All Saints Forum and continues to this day.

The church split was a devastating and painful experience. I was beginning to wonder if I would ever be suited to ministry in a denominational church. Out of the ashes of what appeared like defeat, God birthed a new work that could not otherwise have started.

We held onto the prophetic word not to leave the scene of our trials and resolved to remain and pioneer a new work within the Uniting Church. With the door firmly closed at All Saints, a new and exciting chapter was about to begin.

Lessons Learned   Moving to Australia

COMFORT ZONE

Moving to Australia changed the course of my life. I needed to be taken from my comfort zone so God could get my attention and shape His character in me.

RESEARCH

When accepting a call to a church, it is wise to research the congregation's demographic, history, and your predecessor who left the church.

ALL FOR GOOD

God uses all circumstances for good to those who love Him and are called according to His purposes (Romans 8:28).

CONFLICTS

Jesus taught His disciples to resolve conflicts according to Matthew 18:15-17. Failure to do this resulted in a messy church split.

REFINING

God refines us through a process we find in Romans 5:3-4. Our suffering leads to perseverance, perseverance leads to character, and character leads to hope.

Chapter Three: The Lighthouse and the Tree

The kingdom of heaven is like a mustard seed, which a man took and planted in his field. Though it is the smallest of all your seeds, yet when it grows, it is the largest of garden plants and becomes a tree, so that the birds of the air can come and perch in its branches.

MATTHEW 13: 31-32

The story of Churchlands Christian Fellowship can be divided into three parts, each lasting approximately a decade. The first chapter took place between 1987 and 1998. It was a time of miraculous growth and building momentum. During the second chapter, between 1998 to 2008, growth peaked and we experienced a plateau. During this period, Churchlands developed a new identity and established the Southern Cross Association of Churches. Finally, from 2009 to 2018, Churchlands went through a time of pruning that led to the establishment of Southern Cross Centre.

God lives in trees. Faith is going out on the limbs you think God is telling you to go out on.
JOHN WIMBER

Pioneering a New Work

At the beginning of 1987, the future looked very hopeful. Within a span of six months, our course heading into ministry had completely changed. Having survived the pain of a church split, we were excited at the prospect of pioneering a new work. We now had unprecedented freedom to pursue new paths in renewal and evangelism. We were about to enter a time of growth and building momentum.

Churchlands Christian Fellowship reflects the name of the suburb in Perth where the church began. Churchlands is an area comprised of land originally owned by the Roman Catholic Church. Churchlands was named after a Catholic Bishop purchased land in the area in 1891. Not until the 1980s was the land subdivided and opened to residential development.

In 1987, we entered an agreement with the Churchlands Campus of the WA College of Advanced Education to hire the facilities for up to five years. At the time, our fledgling congregation was made up of about forty adults and twenty children.

Our first church service was held on Sunday, May 3, 1987, in Lecture Theatre One. From that first meeting, we had a strong sense of the Holy Spirit's presence. This, combined with vibrant worship, attracted people who were seeking a deeper walk with the Lord. For the next five years, the congregation would double in size each year. By 1991, over 500 adults were attending our Sunday services.

Like Moses' Journey

Nobody anticipated Churchlands would grow so quickly. I felt inadequate and unprepared for the responsibilities that were increasing. Up to then, I had ministered in established congregations, each with a history and an existing leadership team. Now, we were starting work from scratch.

Even though I had never been in this position before, we felt confident we were exactly in the right place. God had firmly closed one door and opened another. There was no going back. I felt like Moses, leaving Egypt with the newly freed Israelites, on a journey to the land God would show us. Alaine and I gradually came to see that where God guides, He provides.

The Churchlands story is a testimony of God's faithfulness. While things were not always easy, for thirty-two years we witnessed God's miraculous guidance, provision, and protection. People come and go, circumstances change, but the Lord never forgets His promises.

The Lord unfolded a plan that went far beyond what we saw when Churchlands was established. Vision, I came to understand, is given in progressive stages. God's vision is revealed on the journey. We never see the entirety of His plan at the outset.

When I first moved to Perth, I had focused on simply pastoring the All Saints' congregation. I had made a five-year commitment to the church. As the five years came to an end, I sensed that Australia was where God wanted me to continue. I could never have anticipated that our time at All Saints would end with a church split.

When God shuts one door, He opens another. It was never my intent to pioneer a new church in Perth, yet, it was obviously God's plan all along. What I needed, in order to see God's plan, was to arrive at a T-junction.

A T-junction occurs when we face an obstacle and cannot go any further on our previous path. Here we are compelled to make a choice: either we pursue the familiar path or we embark on a new path that requires greater trust in God.

The Lighthouse and the Tree

Watchman Nee, in his book, *Spiritual Authority*, indicates that revelation is the identifying mark of a person who carries spiritual authority. I knew God had given me authority to lead the church, but I still needed revelation to know the way forward.

I was about to discover that what I want and what God gives are two different things. I wanted a detailed road map for the journey ahead, but all God had given me was a compass heading in the form of a lighthouse, a tree, and two scriptures: Matthew 5:14-16 and Matthew 13:31-32.

You are the light of the world. A city on a hill cannot be hidden. Neither do people light a lamp and put it under a bowl. Instead, they put it on its stand, and it gives light to everyone in the house. In the same way, let your light shine before men, that they may see your good deeds and praise your Father in heaven.

Matthew 5:14-16 spoke to me of how Churchlands would become a lighthouse. Lighthouses emit visible beacons to ships, enabling them to safely navigate dangerous waters. The Lord seemed to say that Churchlands would become like a city on a hill, emitting light to everyone in the house.

My immediate thought was that we were to be a lighthouse to the Uniting Church or the City of Perth. I would discover that this was only the beginning.

When Jesus spoke of letting our lights shine before men, He was pointing to the Gospel of the Kingdom of God. Those who inhabit God's Kingdom leave a trail of good deeds that bring praise to our Heavenly Father.

> The kingdom of heaven is like a mustard seed, which a man
> took and planted in his field. Though it is the smallest of all
> your seeds, yet when it grows, it is the largest of garden
> plants and becomes a tree, so that the birds of the air can
> come and perch in its branches.

MATTHEW 13: 31-32

Matthew 13:31-32 tells the parable of the mustard seed. God was indicating that Churchlands was destined to grow and that we needed to prepare to be enlarged. The parable indicates that the Kingdom of God has small beginnings but in time it expands.

While there are many interpretations of "birds of the air" finding shelter, I understood this to be newcomers who would be drawn to the church. Some of whom would build nests in the branches and make Churchlands their spiritual home. Others would rest in the branches, eat some fruit, and then fly away.

The lighthouse and tree became helpful reference points in communicating God's vision and direction for Churchlands. Both pictures accurately depict what would come to pass during Churchlands' thirty-two years of history.

Renewal and Evangelism

Churchlands became a lighthouse and tree by focusing on two priorities: renewal and evangelism. Throughout the twentieth century, churches across the world experienced spiritual awakenings and seasons of renewal. They focused on the person and work of the Holy Spirit. This renewal refers to charismatic renewal. When Churchlands was established in 1987, charismatic renewal evolved into what Dr Peter Wagner called "the third wave", otherwise known as the Neo-charismatic movement.

The first wave of charismatic renewal began in 1901 with the birth of Pentecostalism. The second wave gained momentum in the 1960s impacting mainstream denominational churches. The third wave refers to a subsequent dimension of charismatic renewal that included indigenous and independent groups, such as the Vineyard Movement.

At Churchlands, renewal impacted the church in three areas: 1) worship, 2) the ministry of all believers, and 3) the person and work of the Holy Spirit. Churchlands experienced renewal in each of these areas and resourced other churches who were interested.

Evangelism at Churchlands pointed to power evangelism. Power evangelism differs from traditional evangelism. Traditional evangelism relies heavily on witnessing and persuasion to lead people to Christ. Power evangelism, instead, focuses on demonstrations of God's supernatural power in preparing people to accept Christ. Power evangelism was our primary method of evangelism at Churchlands.

As renewal and evangelism were put into practice, word began to spread that a new Uniting Church with vibrant worship was where the Holy Spirit was moving. At first, people visited our services out of curiosity. Soon they invited their friends.

As the church grew, it was a challenge to keep up. Within months, we needed a children's pastor, then a receptionist, then an office. During this season, the Churchlands elders met every week to pray and discuss developments. God kept us on track to pursue priorities that honored Him: prayer, intimate worship, the ministry of the Holy Spirit, and clear Biblical preaching.

Meeting John Wimber

John Wimber's ministry had a significant impact on the evolution of Churchlands. After attending his conference in Auckland, I was gripped when told he was coming to Australia. In November 1987, John held his first Signs and Wonders and Church Growth conference at Bruce Stadium in Canberra. I gathered a group of about twenty members to attend the conference.

My friend, Dan Armstrong, a Uniting Church pastor, hosted the event. Dan and I had met several years earlier in Iowa. He would eventually assist me in organizing John's conferences in Perth.

On the opening night, I noticed John on the stage doing a sound check. Thinking this might be my only opportunity to speak to him, I gathered up the courage to approach him. After I introduced myself, I asked if he would consider leading a conference in Perth.

I could only imagine what John must have thought. *Perth is so remote, so far away!* However, much to my surprise, he said, "Let's see how this conference goes and we will give it some consideration." I felt peace. I had broken the ice. Now the matter could be left to the Lord.

Looking back, that chance meeting in Canberra with John Wimber changed my life. God gave me amazing favor with John! He was going to become a spiritual father and mentor to Alaine and me.

After the conference, I asked Dan if John had said anything about visiting Perth. Dan replied that things looked hopeful and that it might happen on his next visit to Australia. As the year progressed, "maybe" turned into a "yes". I couldn't believe it! John Wimber was coming to Perth.

Christian Ministries Network

The news of a Signs and Wonders conference with John Wimber sparked great excitement in churches across Western Australia! Perth often missed out on hosting top Christian speakers because of the remote location.

Having never organized a large conference before, I sought Dan's advice. He suggested we invite key Pentecostal and Charismatic leaders across the state to form a board of reference. Within months, we had support from several denominational pastors and leaders, an Anglican bishop, and a few Bible college principals.

The support of this rather eclectic steering group assured maximum participation for the conference. Eventually, this same group became the board of the Christian Ministries Network (CMN) of WA. CMN evolved into a network of ministries. As chairman of CMN, I began meeting regularly with pastors and denominational leaders to plan city-wide events to foster unity and build relationships.

CMN sponsored three of Wimber's conferences, hosted Perth prayer events, and several equipping seminars with high profile speakers. It became a powerful expression of unity across the Body of Christ. Psalm 133 reminds us "Where brethren live in unity, there the Lord commands a blessing".

In CMN, we witnessed authentic and life-changing dimensions of God's power. Eventually, the network expanded to regional cities across WA: Geraldton, Mandurah, Bunbury, Esperance, and Kalgoorlie. All of this was made possible through the dedication and support of our staff and volunteers at Churchlands.

Finding New Premises in Balcatta

By 1991, five years after our meetings commenced at Churchlands College, we had outgrown the venue. We needed a facility that would seat five hundred worshippers on Sundays and where we could host city-wide equipping events.

The Elders felt it was now time to look for a venue within a ten kilometres radius of the college. As our lease agreement was about to expire, there was no time to waste.

I will always remember the rainy Monday morning when I began exploring nearby industrial areas for a building to lease. Nothing looked promising. After several hours, I was getting tired, so I parked in front of a vacant building on Balcatta Road. Exhausted, I began to pray.

Suddenly, I had a strong impression, *You are here. This is the place I have given you!* Opening my eyes, I got out of the car. In front of me stood a huge cream-colored building with a two-storey office at the front and a large factory/warehouse at the rear.

I could not wait to tell Alaine and the Elders! After some research, we discovered the building had housed a window factory, called Vision Windows. The building was constructed in 1982 by a Christian company that went bankrupt. The land alone covered 6,422 square metres. The building had been vacant for two years and the owners were having difficulty in securing a tenant.

The owners wanted a three-year lease, $150,000 for the first year increasing to $190,000 by the third year. For us, this meant a jump in rent from $25,000 to $150,000 a year. Would the Uniting Church oppose the lease? Our only option was to pray. Miraculously, our request to rent was approved by the UCA. Two months later we signed a lease.

This was a huge move for us. Everyone was ecstatic, and an army of volunteers descended on the building to clean and tidy up our new home. After extensive renovations, we held our first service in Balcatta on August 4, 1991.

The future of Churchlands looked bright indeed! We were so grateful for God's miraculous provision just as our lease at the College was about to expire. Once again, however, things were about to change.

Years of Criticism and Trials

Churchlands' relationship with the Uniting Church was rarely amicable. As the church grew, we were criticized and marginalized. Our birth from a church split, links with John Wimber and his bizarre Holy Spirit conferences, plus our general non-conformity with the culture of the UCA, made us a target of criticism.

In spite of this, we honored the prophetic word to "remain in the scene of our trials". We tried, whenever possible, to bless and serve the wider denomination. Churchlands sowed generously into the UCA, both in terms of finances and time.

After seven years of harassment, I was feeling worn down. I remember being accosted by a high-ranking senior minister. He cornered me and snapped, "Why don't you just get out of the Uniting Church? You and your church do not belong! You are not a part of us. Why don't you leave? We don't want you!"

As the years passed, there seemed little chance that we could ever be a lighthouse in the Uniting Church. I believe we made a difference. Some in the Uniting Church recognized that, even if they did not agree with our approach. I perceived we were coming to a T-junction.

The Decision to Leave the Uniting Church

The T-junction came within weeks. I was present at the annual WA Synod meeting. During a report on a private college linked with the church, I sensed the Lord's saying to me, *You have permission to leave.*

My first impression was, *Am I really hearing God?* I shared my impression with the elders. After prayer they agreed. After seven long years, the time had come to cut ties with the UCA and move on.

For our decision to be accepted, the denomination required a congregational meeting and formal vote of the members. This made me a bit uncomfortable, *What if word leaked out that Churchlands was voting to leave the UCA?* Fortunately, my fears were unfounded. When the vote was taken, the final tally was 504 to 4 to leave the UCA.

We then had to communicate the decision to the denominational leaders. It was agreed that Hans Van Wijngaarden, our elders' chairman, and I would meet with two officers of the Presbytery and Synod. The meeting took place in my office.

The day of the meeting, I was nervous but confident we were doing the right thing. The congregation and I had taken a vote to leave the Uniting Church. We hoped to leave as friends and receive a blessing.

When asked why we were leaving, I said we were on the wrong bus. Life for us had been made difficult in the UCA. We could not support the church's views on gay clergy, infant baptism, syncretism, and removing all male references to God from the Bible.

Leaving With a Blessing

Expecting the worst, God intervened by one of the UCA officers present, Beryl Grant, who was a member at All Saints. I had previously served as Beryl's chaplain during her two-year term as moderator of the WA Synod.

I loved Beryl. She was highly respected, gracious, and wise. She said, "John, I know you well enough to know if you've made up your mind, there is little we can do to dissuade you. I want to make your exit from the Uniting Church as smooth as possible."

I was stunned ... and very grateful. We agreed that a service of blessing would be held to recognize our departure. As hoped, we left on good terms and with a blessing. While our departure was a great relief, some of our people were sad because we had been unsuccessful in influencing the direction of the UCA.

I thank God for those seven years, painful as they were. He taught me much about humility and submitting to spiritual authority I did not always agree with. I would soon be tested again in these same areas.

Australian Association of Vineyard Churches Launch

I was unaware that John Wimber had been watching from a distance to see how we departed from the Uniting Church. He told me he was pleased that we had left well and with a blessing.

In April 1994, a year after our departure, John invited Alaine and I to minister with him in Brisbane. He also had something else in mind.

John asked me to become his point man for establishing Vineyard Churches in Australia. I was absolutely delighted!

He also asked me to chair a meeting for him that involved several Australian church leaders. He needed to explain to them that he had wrongly promised a British church leader he would not plant Vineyard Churches in Australia. He now believed his promise was invalid and that God had now given him permission.

Several months later, in February 1995, John travelled to Perth to launch the Australian Association of Vineyard Churches. The launch was held at Churchlands and was attended by dozens of pastors from across Australia.

Out of many hopefuls, only eleven pastors were invited to join Vineyard. I was disappointed because the selection process seemed very disorganized. There was no plan or solid criteria for selecting members. The result was messy, eleven pastors thrown together and told to behave like a family.

National and International Vineyard Office

As John's point man, I had the task of setting up a national office. We needed to develop methods of communicating, organizing national leaders' events, and establishing a budget. It was agreed that expenses would be met from member churches contributing a percentage of their income to the Australian Association.

John felt restrained to appoint an Australian national leader at this point. He wanted to see who would rise up. In the interim, two pastors were appointed to oversee Vineyard Churches in Australia. I became the regional overseer for WA and South Australia. David Owens from Sydney was to oversee churches in Queensland, New South Wales, and Victoria.

David struggled to build cohesion in the Sydney pastors. This only got worse with time. Believing Australian Vineyard pastors to be an unruly group, US Vineyard took charge. The situation in Sydney became so frustrating that I requested a meeting in Anaheim with John. Unfortunately, no action came from the meeting and the situation continued to deteriorate.

During our four years in Vineyard, Alaine and I were grateful to John for inviting us to the annual meetings of the Vineyard International Consortium (VIC). VIC was a training ground for future national leaders of the movement. John Wimber's presence was the glue that held VIC together, as I was about to discover.

John Wimber's Death

By 1997, John's health was deteriorating. He told us he would not be around for much longer. He died in November 1997 at the age of 63. I attended John's funeral. It was a fitting tribute to a great 'equipper of the saints.' Prior to John's funeral, I felt something unsettling in the atmosphere surrounding the event, like change was in the wind.

Unlike many Vineyard leaders, Alaine and I were affiliated with Vineyard because of our close relationship with John Wimber. We knew John during the final decade of his life. This could have played a part in what happened next.

In June 1998, Alaine and I were invited to the annual VIC meeting at the Wimber holiday home in the mountains outside Los Angeles. There seemed to us a heaviness hanging over the meetings. When I raised the subject of the five-fold ministry (see Ephesians 4:11), I soon discovered I had hit on a sore subject. From then, we felt people were avoiding us.

Late on the final evening of VIC, a proposal was put forward that the New Zealand national leader appointed should lead Vineyard in Australia. This came as a surprise as there had been no prior consultation on the matter.

Seeing another disaster in the making, I questioned the proposal. It was late at night, and everyone was exhausted. What followed next was sad. A top leader in the movement rebuked me publicly for thinking that I could ever be a leader in Vineyard.

Fortunately, Alaine and I had prayed fervently before the meeting. We pleaded with God to show us the way forward, as our four years in Vineyard had been so frustrating.

Alaine and I were asked to meet with the VIC leaders the following morning. As we entered the room, the leaders were present but their wives were absent. All eyes were looking down.

One of the national leaders then spoke, "John, we think you are a good leader but not the kind of leader we're looking for in Vineyard." The same leader who had spoken the night before, again interjected, "You'll never be a leader in Vineyard."

In shock, I asked, "Does this mean you want us to leave the Vineyard?" The response was, "Oh no, you don't have to leave the Vineyard. We just want you to know you will never be a leader in Vineyard." To me, however, the message was quite clear. We had been shown the door.

Leaving the Vineyard

Driving down the mountain back to LA was a sombre occasion. We had served John and Vineyard and had tried to lay good foundations for the movement in Australia. We were hurt and in shock!

Even then, I knew that God must have a purpose in allowing me to be publicly humiliated. I whispered to Alaine, "God must have something amazing in store that He would so decisively remove us from the Vineyard."

News quickly spread of our fall from grace. This brought diverse reactions from friends and colleagues. Everyone knew how much we had invested in Vineyard and how much we loved John Wimber.

Two months later, a meeting was held at Churchlands in which it was announced that I had been officially removed from Vineyard leadership. The group were told that anyone who wanted to remain under my leadership would be asked to leave Vineyard.

God had clearly closed a door. Our decision to leave the Vineyard was supported by most of the congregation. There were others who decided now was their time to move on.

So deep was our disappointment that it took two years for our wounds to heal. Now we can see the redemptive purposes of God in this amazing series of events. Some of life's greatest lessons can be learned only through pain. I needed to die to my flesh and my ego.

We believe God led us into the Vineyard and we will always be grateful to John Wimber. He embraced Alaine and I when we were young and inexperienced. He exposed us to the inner workings of an international association of churches.

I believe John Wimber heard from God when he didn't install us as Australian national leaders of Vineyard. Even though he knew our future lay elsewhere, he included us in his inner circle anyway. We will always be grateful for his kindness toward us.

Purchasing 154 Balcatta Road

Alaine and I once again sought the Lord about our way forward. Churchlands appeared to be in a good position. In the short space of eleven years, the church had grown to nearly 1500 adherents. We had twenty-five full and part-time staff. We had survived the departure from Vineyard with minimal losses.

After leasing our building for seven years, the owners decided to sell the property. We had a considerable investment in the building and had carried out many renovations. The owners' asking price was just over two million dollars.

We had two options, purchase the building or take a chance we could continue to lease from the new owners. After prayer, we felt the Lord leading us to purchase the building.

Two million dollars is a lot of money. The elders felt it wise to pay off the debt as quickly as possible.

After prayer we embarked on a project called A Time to Build. Every family unit in the church would be asked to make a one-off contribution and/or pledge an amount over a two-year period.

After three months of preparation, the big day came when the offering was to be taken. It was quite touching to see individuals and families come forward and place their offerings in the two large baskets.

When the offering was counted, over one million dollars had been given in cash and an additional $500,000 was pledged over the next two years. We were overwhelmed at God's gracious provision!

In faith, we had gone out on a limb by signing the purchase agreement before the offering was taken. We needed tools to do the work of God and He had graciously provided. We now owned a venue where we could host conferences and other events to equip the saints across our city. The purchase of 154 Balcatta Road was a huge victory.

CONCLUSION

Spiritual covering. God uses paradoxical and often painful situations to shape His character in us. For a decade, Churchlands was under the spiritual covering of two very different organizations: The Uniting Church and the Vineyard Movement. God used both groups to teach us enduring lessons.

Honoring the Uniting Church. I will likely be remembered in the Uniting Church as a 'larrikin'. I did not conform and tried to be true to my convictions. In spite of our, at times, tense relationship, I honor the Uniting Church for two reasons. One, the denomination welcomed me as a pastor from the US sight unseen, otherwise I might never have moved to Australia. Two, if Perth Presbytery had not intervened at All Saints, Churchlands might never have been established. God used the Uniting Church to shape the course of my life and ministry.

Australian Christianity. I learned a great deal about Australian Christianity during my thirteen years in the Uniting Church. For five years, I was saturated in its history, theology, and mission as I did my research. I had access to three of the architects of the UCA: Winston O'Reiley (Methodist), David Oxley (Congregational), and Davis McCaughey (Presbyterian). I also had interviewed thirty former Presbyterian, Methodist, Congregationalist pastors, and lay leaders from across Western Australia. My association with the Uniting Church helped me better understand the role of the church in Australian society.

Vineyard. In stark contrast to the UCA, our association with John Wimber exposed us to the vibrant Neo-charismatic movement. He carried a unique gifting in worship, teaching, and demonstrating the power of God. We learned so much from our close friendship with John. When he died, our association with Vineyard ceased. Vineyard, like any organization, had great strengths and some weaknesses. Looking back, if we had remained in Vineyard, we would never have embarked on our next great adventure. We are grateful for our four years in the Vineyard.

Lessons Learned   The Lighthouse and the Tree

REVELATION

Revelation is the quality seen in a person who carries God-given spiritual authority.

VISION

Vision is often revealed in progressive stages. We never see God's full plan at the outset of one's assignment. It is revealed on the journey.

DEATH OF FOUNDER

Movements and denominations change when their founder dies.

SUBMISSION

We can learn many lessons by submitting to authority we do not always agree with.

PAIN TEACHES US

Life's greatest lessons are learned through pain.

COMPASS HEADING

God never gives us a detailed road map of what lies ahead, only a compass heading.

PART TWO: THE
JOURNEY

CHAPTER FOUR: UNDER THE SOUTHERN CROSS

Enlarge the place of your tent. Stretch your tent curtains wide, do not hold back; lengthen your cords, strengthen your stakes. For you will spread out to the right and to the left;

ISAIAH 54:2-3a

The Lord revealed a new dimension of the lighthouse and the tree as Churchlands became the 'mother church' of a network of ministries. The Southern Cross Association of Churches had small beginnings and would eventually span nations across the Southern Hemisphere. In this chapter, we follow the formation, growth, and expansion of Southern Cross as a model for Biblical community, equipping and deploying the saints for the work of ministry.

If God shuts one door, He
opens another.
IRISH PROVERB

Lessons from Astronomy

One of my hobbies is astronomy. In my early teens, I delivered newspapers early every morning, 365 days a year. While it was still dark, I would often stop at my old primary school playground to contemplate the beauty of the heavens. Gazing upward, I would ask God what He had planned for my future.

When I was sixteen, I built my first telescope, an eight-inch Newtonian reflector. I assembled the scope from parts bought with the money from delivering newspapers. Little did I imagine that someday I would be living in Australia, a nation where the constellation of the Southern Cross is always visible at night.

The Southern Cross constellation is also called *Crux*, which is Latin for cross. It is unique in that two of its brightest stars point to the South Celestial Pole, an important reference point in astronomy and navigation. The Southern Cross constellation is a symbol of hope. The Southern Cross logo appears on the national flags of Australia, New Zealand, and Brazil.

When we look at Crux, we consider the Lord's promise to Abraham in Genesis 15:5. Abraham is the father of all who live by faith. We who follow Christ are spiritual sons of Abraham. I chose this symbol as the name of an association of churches that, the Lord revealed, would one day link Christian leaders from across the Southern Hemisphere.

Look up at the heavens and count the stars—if indeed you can count them. Then He said to him, "And so shall your offspring be."

GENESIS 15:5

The Vision

As Alaine and I prayed about our future post-Vineyard, I was reminded of a vision I had several years earlier. In the vision, seven power pylons were arranged in a circle, connected by wires sagging between them. I noticed several hands reaching up from the soil and taking hold of the sagging wires.

The Lord then spoke, *This is a vision of the future. You are one of the seven pylons. The remaining six are ministries who will link with you. As the seven ministries stand together, others will draw strength from the unity that exists between you.*

At first, I thought the vision pertained to Perth. Gradually, it dawned on me that the revelation had a wider, future application.

Vineyard 'Old Boys' Club

One day, I unexpectedly received an email from a Namibian pastor. I had met him at a conference in South Africa a few years earlier. He heard we had recently left Vineyard and was in a similar situation. He then asked, "Do you think we should start a Vineyard 'old boys' club?"

God often speaks in unexpected ways. His unusual question started me thinking, "*A Vineyard 'old boys' club?*" Yes, many were touched by John Wimber's ministry, but never had become part of the Vineyard Movement.

I ran the idea by Dan Armstrong and John Blacker, two senior Aussie statesmen in charismatic renewal. I then spoke with pastor friends, John Gilmour, Tom Quinlivan, and Alex Harrower. All were favorable to pursuing the matter.

Looking at my diary, I was due to visit Nairobi in July. I thought that since I will already be in Africa, I could divert to Windhoek on the way back to Perth. Windhoek, the Namibian capital, was just a two-hour flight from Johannesburg. I sensed the meeting could be significant.

According to plan, Pastor Bruce Mulder met me at Windhoek International Airport. We immediately connected. As we shared stories from Vineyard days, I knew this was no ordinary meeting. I found Bruce to be visionary, passionate, and forceful. We both had a passion for equipping and had much in common.

The Formation of Southern Cross

After a couple of days, I suggested to Bruce we hold an international gathering in Perth and bring together some of the 'old boys' who had been touched by Wimber's ministry. We agreed to invite five close colleagues to join us in the hope of establishing a link between Australia and Africa. Returning to Perth, I contacted my friends and shared what had happened in Namibia. They too sensed that God was birthing something new.

On March 7, 1999, six pastors and myself, five from Australia and two from Africa, met at Churchlands to launch the Southern Cross Association of Churches (SCAC). The founding group consisted of Bruce Mulder (Windhoek, Namibia), Dan Armstrong (Toronto, NSW), John Blacker (Melbourne, Victoria), John Gilmour (Perth), Tom Quinlivan (Perth), Alex Harrower (Cape Town, South Africa), and John McElroy (Perth).

I put together an introductory brochure to distribute at the event. It summarized a vision that God was showing me for this group:

> "The vision (of Southern Cross) is to establish a network of ministries to build bridges of encouragement between Christian leaders through the Southern Hemisphere. John McElroy's perception is that everybody in ministry had something important to 'bring to the table'.
>
> Southern Cross is a place of mutual encouragement, where large and small ministries, Pentecostals and Evangelicals, black and white, young and old can work together and learn from each other. Our vision is to see the church united in its

diversity, non-competitive, generous to those who need help and encouragement, not empire building but Kingdom building."

Fulfilment of the Vision

The seven ministries who came together in Perth fulfilled my earlier vision of seven power pylons in a circle. Through the relationship between the seven, dozens of ministries linked with us to receive encouragement and be equipped for the work of ministry.

Our relationship was strengthened by seven values we shared: the Bible, prayer, unity, equipping, spiritual parenting, empowering relationships, and freedom in Christ. These values continue to guide Southern Cross as it moves forward. From the outset, we shared the desire to be part of an inclusive, safe family of ministries. We resolved:

+ To welcome all Christian leaders, be inclusive, and embrace men and women from all racial, denominational, and cultural backgrounds.

+ We would not compete with other networks, movements, or denominations, but would maintain a Kingdom focus on unity and cooperation.

+ Although called an "Association of Churches", Southern Cross membership would be open to anyone in Christian ministry, whether they were serving in churches, parachurch organizations, or marketplaces.

+ Members would agree to high standards of integrity, character, and behaviour.

+ Membership would be for a one-year, renewable period. People should not feel 'locked in' to membership if circumstances change or they wish to join another group.

+ The costs of membership would be kept minimal by using the services of our church for administration and conferences.

Growth from Small Beginnings

Word of SCAC spread slowly at first, mainly through personal friends of the seven original members. As news of SCAC spread, I received invitations to speak to pastors and church leaders across Australia and Africa.

We soon discovered that many pastors had no grid for understanding a network based on relationships. Our first priority was to build working models of groups that reflected our values. This gave rise to establishing regional cluster groups. We continue to pursue the vision the Lord gave us. Our seven values remain unchanged.

We chose to establish the first regional clusters in the cities where we already had significant support: Perth, Adelaide, and Windhoek. I facilitated the group in Perth, Brian Chalmers in Adelaide, and Bruce Mulder in Windhoek. We began small, inviting friends and other interested people to join in half-day equipping and fellowship events. Before long, small clusters were meeting a few times a year in each area.

As word of SCAC spread, other groups started in Melbourne, Sydney, and Cape Town. These groups were facilitated by John Blacker, Pete Wilson, and Alex Harrower. My goal was to visit each group at least once a year. On my visits, I would teach on leadership and share ministry stories I had learned on my travels or at Churchlands.

First Australian National Leaders' Advance

From past experience, I knew the importance of bringing leaders together for local and national gatherings. In March 2000, a year after our first event in Perth, we held an Australian National Leaders' Advance in Victor Harbor, South Australia.

The format was simple. We would arrive on Friday night for a meet and greet evening. Mornings and afternoons on Saturday and Sunday were devoted to teaching and business sessions. The late afternoons and evenings were left free to relax and minister to each other. The Australian National Leaders' Advance would rotate each year between South Australia, Victoria, Tasmania, New South Wales, and Queensland.

In addition to the annual Leaders' Advance, we introduced other services to our members: ordination and official endorsement of ministries, Apostolic consultations, cutting edge resources, and the opportunity to be part of a regional support group. As we are registered by the Australian Government as an official denomination, we are able to nominate our members as official marriage celebrants.

SCAC in Africa

While SCAC was spreading across Australia, other regional leaders' groups commenced in Namibia and Mauritius. SCAC eventually linked with pastors in Zambia, Angola, the Democratic Republic of Congo, Seychelles, and Kenya.

In 2008, I ordained Apostle Busisiwe Thebehali in Soweto, South Africa. Busisiwe has become a spiritual daughter to Alaine and me. Each year, she hosts an apostolic school under her banner of Agape Christian Ministries. Agape Ministries connects pastors across sub-Saharan Africa.

SCAC's work in Kenya has also grown significantly. This is due to the efforts of Jody Pike, David Apelt, Julie Shannon, and Anthony and Fiona Schopf. For over a decade, we hosted SCAC Leaders' Advances in Nairobi, focusing on ten Kenyan couples in ministry. In 2019, SCAC East Africa was launched with the appointment of the first SCAC indigenous Kenyan National Leader, Bishop John Wandera.

SCAC's expansion in Africa reflected a pattern similar to Paul's missionary journeys in the Book of Acts. First, I travelled to Africa by myself or was accompanied by one or two colleagues. Next, we organized small ministry teams to visit strategic cities. As we discovered where we have favor, we have focused our time and resources building into key leaders. We now have narrowed our focus to equipping in Africa to Soweto, Nairobi, and Mauritius.

Lessons from Africa

The Lord has taught us several lessons in thirty years of ministering in Africa:

Raise up and release indigenous leaders. In SCAC, we have resolved to leave a small leadership footprint in Africa and have focused on raising up and releasing indigenous leaders. African leaders have often adopted models and the culture of Western Pentecostals, Catholics, and other missionary denominations. Some of these practices and cultures can be irrelevant and unhelpful in the African context.

Avoid the pitfalls of tribalism and paternalism. *Tribalism* is the practice of a pastor acting like a tribal chief, ruling over the church and being reluctant to raise up and release new leaders outside of their family. African leaders need encouragement to 'pass on the baton' of leadership outside their immediate families, and to apprentices. *Paternalism* involves handing out money to indigenous ministries or keeping them financially dependent on a movement or denomination. This perpetuates a 'handout' mentality that inhibits financially self-sustaining churches.

Teach and shape truly Biblical and apostolic church culture. Many African church leaders have strong evangelistic gifts but are weak in teaching and understanding the full counsel of God's Word. This leads to error, excessive practices, and division. Africa needs indigenous leaders who are able to plant churches that are apostolically-configured.

SCAC Expands to South America

When SCAC began in 1999, the Lord impressed on me that SCAC

would eventually expand into South America. At that time, I had never travelled there and knew only one couple from Salta, Argentina.

This couple introduced me to Eduardo Lorenzo, a significant figure in the Argentinian revival following the Falklands War. Eduardo was head of the Baptist Churches of Argentina. He welcomed me to visit and speak in his church in Adrogue, a regional city south of Buenos Aires.

On three occasions, I ministered in Adrogue and met some key Argentine leaders involved in the revival. I was grateful for the opportunity to learn from these wonderful saints. Many of the Argentinian leaders already had strong links to the US and other nations. Feeling that a door had closed, I continued to focus on SCAC in Australia, Africa, and Mauritius.

Two years later, I met Pastor Rodrigo Guerra, a former Christian Outreach Centre pastor from Santiago, Chile. He invited us to minister in his church. Rodrigo was keen to develop links with SCAC and saw it as an opportunity to develop his apostolic focus in Chile and other surrounding nations. Rodrigo has subsequently visited Australia twice and has established a small but vibrant Chilean branch of SCAC.

In 2015, I was introduced to Pastor Rogerio Olimpio from Sao Paulo, Brazil. Rogerio is a business coach and trainer in a business leadership school called The Five Capitals. He is a gifted and energetic leader and mentor to several young church leaders. Rogerio and his wife, Estela, have recently been appointed as national leaders of SCAC in Brazil. In 2019, the first SCAC conference was held in Sao Paulo with over a hundred participants.

South America is the third and final continent in the Southern Hemisphere to link with Southern Cross. We are encouraged by the cluster leadership emerging in Sao Paulo and Santiago. Rodrigo and Rogerio are capable indigenous leaders committed to apostolic reformation and building SCAC in their respective nations.

CONCLUSION

Healthy growth. In two decades, Southern Cross has grown to include over two hundred Christian leaders across the Southern Hemisphere. Now recognized as a denomination by the Australian Government, SCAC has regional convenors in Australia, Africa, and South America. It continues to grow on all three continents as members share positive stories with friends and colleagues across seventeen nations.

Apostolic nature. Southern Cross, while called an "Association of Churches", includes men and women in a variety of church, community, and marketplace ministry settings. Our cohesion stems from embracing seven shared values: the Bible, prayer, unity, equipping, spiritual parenting, empowering relationships, and freedom in Christ.

Teaching and equipping. As Director of Southern Cross, I travel to strategic cities to teach and equip our members in the principles of apostolic ministry. SCAC has now become a significant advocate for apostolic reformation in the Southern Hemisphere. The relationships and trust that have developed between members over the past two decades, provides a conduit for sharing resources between nations and continents.

Membership. SCAC membership has numerous benefits. After joining the network, membership is renewable on a yearly basis. A copy of the Southern Cross Informational Brochure is available via a link in the "Extra Material" section at the end of the book.

Local church support. From the outset, the Southern Cross Association of Churches has been enabled by the elders of Churchlands Christian Fellowship releasing me to serve the wider Body of Christ as Director of SCAC. The foundational work of Churchlands continues through Southern Cross Centre (SCC). The original vision of the lighthouse and the tree is being fulfilled by the Southern Cross Association of Churches.

Lessons Learned   Under the Southern Cross

DISCERNING SEASONS

When God closes one door, He opens another. Wisdom is knowing when one spiritual season has finished and how to position for the new season.

MISSIONARY JOURNEYS

There is a parallel between Paul's three missionary journeys and the way SCAC was established. First, individuals were sent. Next, teams were sent. Gradually, we have strategically held conferences and established equipping centres in cities.

GROWTH

The first members of SCAC were attracted to a new church wineskin based on relationship, encouragement, and equipping. As SCAC regional groups were established, members began to share positive testimonies and the network grew significantly.

EQUIPPING FROM EXPERIENCE

My effectiveness in leading a network has been enhanced by remaining pastor of a local church. Many of the lessons I continue to share with SCAC leaders have arisen from the crucible of hands-on ministry.

OPPOSITION

Five-fold equippers in pastoral ministry may face local opposition to the concept of ministry to the wider Body of Christ. I faced opposition from church members.

VISION

Church leaders are crying out for spiritual fathers and mothers. One becomes a spiritual father or mother by first being a spiritual son or daughter.

CHAPTER FIVE: A CULTURE OF SONSHIP

Your attitude should be the same as Jesus: Who, being in
very nature God, did not consider equality with God
something to be grasped, but made himself nothing, taking
the very nature of a servant, being made in human likeness.

PHILIPPIANS 2:5-7

*Following a decade of rapid growth, Churchlands entered a season of
plateau when numbers and momentum began to level off. After leaving
Vineyard we needed to reinvent ourselves and pursue a new identity. The
loss of previous growth and momentum brought to the surface tensions
and character issues in our leadership team. During this time, I wrote a
book entitled,* Passing on the Baton. *The book highlights the importance
of developing a culture of sonship in the local church. During this season,
God began to show me that only spiritual sons and daughters are
capable of building a strong local church.*

To have a spirit of sonship is to put
yourself underneath another's mission
and do all you can to make them
successful, knowing that as a son or
daughter, there is an inheritance that
lies ahead.

JACK FROST

50

Culture of Honor

What is a culture of sonship? Jesus was the obedient Son of a loving Father. Jesus honored others above Himself. He honored His Heavenly Father by submitting to His will. The Father honored the Son. Jesus honored His disciples by washing their feet.

A culture of sonship is a culture of honor. We honor others whenever we show them respect and behave in a way that adds value to their lives. When we honor others, we follow in the footsteps of Jesus.

In Mark 3:25, Jesus said, "If a house is divided against itself, that house cannot stand." As Churchlands progressed from rapid growth to a phase of plateau, cracks appeared in the relationships that held our leadership team in unity and singularity of vision. These cracks can be traced to a lack of honor and to fear, envy, and selfish ambition.

When we fail to build leadership teams on Jesus' foundation of sonship, we perpetuate an orphan spirit that works against unity, teamwork, and true Biblical community in the local church.

The Buck Stops Here

On the desk of US President Harry Truman was a plaque that read, "*THE BUCK STOPS HERE!*" Truman was a stickler for honesty and had a no-nonsense approach to leadership. 'Passing the buck' means not taking responsibility for our mistakes and blaming others. Good leaders admit their mistakes and take responsibility for their poor decisions. They are humble and ask for forgiveness when others are hurt by their actions.

While I have made many mistakes, one stands out to me: I sometimes hired or promoted difficult people into church leadership. While they may have presented well at first, it soon became apparent that I had made a mistake. Either they lacked spiritual maturity, required constant management, lacked self-initiative, or pursued their own goals at the expense of others. God was teaching me that only spiritual sons and daughters are able to build the house of God.

God was merciful by not allowing me to succumb to my poor choices. Instead, He allowed me to reap the fruit of my decisions. He taught me that more mistakes are made by impatience rather than by waiting. I needed to be more prayerful, consultative, cautious, and confrontational. As Senior Pastor, the buck stopped with me.

I once had a basketball coach who said, "Life's greatest lessons are learned not from winning, but when we lose the game." After years of rapid success and growing significance, I had to face the reality that Churchlands was starting to plateau. During this season, five events reinforced why it is crucial to establish a culture of sonship in churches:

- The purchase of 154 Balcatta Road.

- Wise advice from a prophet.

- The marriage breakup of a close colleague.

- Staff challenges.

- The sale of our church building.

The Decision to Purchase Our Building

While the purchase of 154 Balcatta Road in 1998 was a great victory, it also led to some unforeseen problems. After the purchase, there was a subtle shift in the attitude of some of our volunteer leaders. They were growing weary and wanted the paid staff to find replacements for them.

The first sign of a church plateau was the decreasing energy and enthusiasm among volunteers. We now struggled to find willing workers to serve in the ministries of the church. This led to a destructive practice called 'plug and play'. 'Plug and play' means finding someone willing to serve, plugging them quickly into a position, and hoping it works. Unfortunately, this practice usually creates more problems than it solves.

One of the drawbacks of having paid staff is that people begin to assume someone else is paid to do the job. This problem is compounded when staff are unwilling or unable to raise up apprentices. There can be various reasons for this. Sometimes staff want to protect their jobs. At other times they may want to keep others dependent on them, so they do most of the work themselves.

I now see that these attitudes can be symptomatic of an orphan spirit. John Maxwell once made the observation, "A leader who raises followers needs to be needed. A leader who raises up leaders wants to be succeeded." He also said, "You can't lead people if you need people." By this, he meant you cannot make tough decisions or give strong leadership if you constantly require the affirmation of those you lead.

There is a distinct difference between the motivations of those simply paid to do a job, and spiritual sons and daughters. Employees are paid to do a job. Sons and daughters want to build the house. A culture of sonship produces secure leaders who can multiply themselves. When our building was purchased in 1998, we had little awareness of the importance of sonship.

Our awareness of a culture of sonship started with the 2006 release of my book, *Passing on The Baton*. As energy and enthusiasm decreased and cracks began to appear, I began to see the need for changes in our leadership culture. Only spiritual sons and daughters can build the house of God. This would soon be confirmed by Graham Cooke.

Graham Cooke's 2008 Conference at Churchlands

I first met Graham Cooke, an acclaimed prophet and author, through a friend's introduction in Sydney. Graham told me he never accepted speaking "invitations", but only "assignments" from the Lord. If Graham agreed to come to Perth, I knew it would be because the Lord had spoken to him. When I invited him to speak, he accepted without hesitation. We asked him to address the subject of "Living the Kingdom".

The first night Graham spoke, we had a strong sense of God's presence. With every eye rivetted, he declared the purpose of his ministry was to war against the religious spirit. Graham was clear and to the point: God is doing a new thing. Do not cling to the past. The Lord is about to do the unexpected!

I had the strong impression Graham's message was directed specifically at me. He focused on three words: *favor, acceleration,* and *prototype*. We were about to experience the Lord's favor like never before. Graham repeated the word "favor" for what seemed like a hundred times to emphasize the point. To know God's favor, we must understand our identity in Christ.

Graham then emphasized that a season of *acceleration* was coming soon. God's purposes for us were about to accelerate. Things that normally took years would now take months. Things that took months would take weeks. Things that took weeks would take days. Things that took days would happen in hours. In my spirit, I perceived that this pointed to cooperating with God's purposes. When we see what the Father is doing, and cooperate, His will comes to pass sooner than if we resist.

Finally, Graham proclaimed that a new *prototype* was about to be launched in Perth. This really caught my attention. Graham did not say much about the prototype, but he made it clear, it would be something totally new.

After the conference, on the way to the airport, I asked Graham what I could do to "pastor the prototype"; to help it emerge. His answer was simply, "Work with those who support your vision and want to move ahead with you". I now realize what Graham meant: I needed to build with spiritual sons and daughters. As Graham boarded his flight, an event was about to occur that would catapult us into turmoil.

A Painful Lesson

A month after Graham's departure, Alaine and I were preparing for a holiday break. On Saturday morning, four days before Christmas, the phone rang. Alaine answered. I could hear a woman in great distress, shouting, "*I've caught them, I've caught them!*" The woman was the wife of our executive pastor, Ron Ings.

Ron had just been caught by his wife in the arms of another woman! The woman was the wife of a visiting pastor. Ron was a close friend who served my vision like a spiritual son for over fifteen years. His presence brought stability to the church whenever I was away from Perth. We were about to witness the end of two marriages, involving four of our closest friends.

I had never faced a situation like this. My immediate thoughts were about damage control. People knew that Ron was like a spiritual son to me. I needed to communicate transparently and hopefully quash any gossip or malicious rumours that could divide the church.

I was about to learn a painful lesson. When a church leader falls, it gives the enemy an opportunity to attack the congregation. This attack came in the form of a spirit of accusation that would manifest in Churchlands for many years. Criticisms began to surface, and I wondered why they were being directed at me.

Reflecting on the loss of our executive pastor, could I have been a better spiritual father? Could I have been a better listener? Should I have probed more into his personal life, marriage, and walk with the Lord? Could I have been a better mentor, coach, motivator, and example to Ron?

Much of our interaction was based on leading the church and decision making. We also related closely at a social level. I will never know if being a better spiritual father would have changed the outcome of Ron's marriage. Through this painful experience, I became aware of the need for a deeper level of transparency with those closest to me.

When God allows a shaking, His purposes are always redemptive. The accusations and criticisms alerted me again to the apparent superficiality of our church culture. When things go wrong, someone has to bear the blame. That someone turned out to be me. I knew I was being pruned so I could become more fruitful, John 15:2 "He (the Father) cuts off every branch in me that bears no fruit, while every branch that does bear fruit, He prunes so that it will be even more fruitful."

We judge others on whether they get things right. God looks at how we respond when things go wrong. Sometimes we want to run from the scene of our trials or put the blame on someone else. Had I become more focused on outcomes than relationships? The breakup of my colleague's marriage forced me to re-evaluate my priorities and the leadership culture of our church.

Staff Challenges

My greatest challenge as a senior pastor has been in selecting and overseeing paid staff. Managing and holding others accountable for their use of time is not one of my natural strengths. As a visionary, I need the assistance of people with management skills and the capacity to oversee the work of paid staff.

I have learned that paid staff and key volunteers should be selected only after a period of observation. They also need adequate training. Before appointing leaders, we should always consider the four *C*s: *calling*, *chemistry*, *competence*, and *character*.

Calling is our God-given assignment. Knowing our assignment and that of others enables teamwork and placing people in the right position.

Chemistry is about relational cohesion and getting along with others. For a team to function well, they should enjoy working together and be able to celebrate the successes of others.

Competence points to the skills and training required to perform our assignment well. We need skills commensurate to our job. Spiritual sons and daughters will often start out awkwardly and improve with time. Competence improves with experience, instruction, supervision, and being teachable.

Character essentially points to the fruit of the Spirit found in Galatians 5:22-23. Character is what differentiates spiritual sons from orphans. Sons are secure in their future. They are loyal to the established leaders. Orphans are insecure and end up using their position for selfish purposes. They struggle with loyalty to leadership because they have their own agendas.

During the growth phase of a church, when momentum is strong, character flaws are easily hidden. In times of plateau or decline, cracks begin to surface. When character flaws are exposed, we have two choices: we can attempt to deal with them, or we can run away.

When leaders leave a church, their followers often move on as well. When staff left Churchlands, we would customarily honor and endeavour to speak well of them. Sometimes this was not reciprocated. When leaving an organization, we should always be gracious in what we share. Negativity and "faint praise" cause people to stumble. Hebrews 12:15, "See to it that no one misses the grace of God and that no bitter root grows up to cause trouble and defile many."

My experience of working with church staff and volunteers reveal there are four essential qualities of a spiritual son or daughter: integrity, loyalty to the senior leader, being a team player (not independent), and a good work ethic. These are the qualities of true spiritual sons and daughters.

The Sale of 154 Balcatta Road

By early 2017, the costs associated with maintaining our building were becoming difficult to sustain. We no longer needed a large facility. After exploring options for re-development, the elders concluded we should sell and downsize. A property valuation was approved and conducted but the elders felt to hold off actually placing the property on the market just yet.

Within days of the valuation, a pastor phoned my office for an appointment. He indicated we had never met, but he was senior leader of a large church in the northern suburbs. He said the Lord had spoken to him about purchasing our building and wondered whether we might consider selling. I said we had recently completed a valuation and were favorable to discussing the matter.

A meeting was scheduled for leaders of both churches. The chairman of the CCF elders, Fred Boshart, and I attended the meeting. When queried about our asking price, their leaders accepted our request without hesitation. An agreement was then signed to finalize the sale by December 2018.

The process happened very quickly, too quickly apparently, for two of our seven elders. Although an agreement had been signed, they now felt uncomfortable about the sale. I had been led to believe that we had the unanimous support of the Elders. My heart sank at the prospect of not being able to present a united front on this important issue. To make matters worse, the two elders then resigned in protest.

Predictably, we faced division in the congregation over the sale of the building. Alaine and I faced insult and accusation. It was like we were being blamed and punished for needing to sell the building. The level of dishonor was of great concern. Finally, it began to dawn on me that our elders were not relationally or apostolically-configured. We had simply repeated the model used in the Uniting Church.

Elders in New Testament churches were selected and mentored by apostles. They had outstanding character (see 1 Timothy 3:1-7) and relationally were like spiritual sons and daughters to an apostle. Once the elders had been trained, the apostolic overseer kept in regular contact and was a sounding board as required. When important issues arose, the apostle had the authority to exhort, correct, or rebuke.

While events surrounding the sale of 154 Balcatta Road were difficult, they brought to the surface issues we needed to address.

CONCLUSION

During the plateau phase of Churchlands, the Lord revealed our need to develop a culture of honor. The CEO, employee, eldership model of leadership we had inherited was flawed. What we needed was a leadership model that was more Biblical, honoring, and relationally based.

Gratitude precedes honor. A culture of sonship is, above all, a culture of honor. We honor others whenever we show respect or behave in a way that adds value to their life. Honor arises from *gratitude* in our hearts. It can never be forced and can only be given willingly.

Gratitude feeds the desire to honor others above ourselves. Honor comes from the realization that another person has enabled you to achieve something you could not have done without them. It is this realization that makes us grateful and releases love and humility in our hearts.

Honor is often missing in the church. People are quick to criticise or dishonor others if their behavior is challenged, or a decision is made that they misunderstand or disagree with. Many of us are unaware of the sacrifices others continually make for our benefit behind the scenes.

To restore honor in the church, we need more of God's grace and to create a deeper sense of Christian community. Community is built on relationship with God and each other. We see models of community in the New Testament that can assist us in recapturing the love dynamic that was present among early Christians.

Healthy heart. When it comes to establishing healthy churches, only spiritual sons and daughters can build the house of God. We must examine our hearts. Are we behaving like a son or an orphan? To assist us, we present the following diagram:

The Heart of a Son	The Heart of an Orphan
Sons build the house.	Orphans serve in the house out of duty, doing only what they have to.
Sons hold the father's vision as their own and seek to accomplish it.	Orphans serve only the parts of the vision that they like.
Sons speak by using family language, we, our, us, to one another.	Orphans use individual terminology: me, my, I, mine.
Sons are family-oriented.	Orphans are issue oriented—being right is most important, resulting in splitting over issues.
Sons will submit to the Father's authority.	Orphans frequently question decisions.
Sons will build into the lives of others and want to pass on their baton to others.	Orphans keep people dependent on them and will not pass on their baton to others.
Sons bond newcomers into the family.	Orphans gather new people to themselves.

The Heart of a Son	The Heart of an Orphan
Sons focus on serving and on the well-being of other people.	Orphans focus on appearances and how to look good.
Sons are transparent—they share their inner thoughts and feelings.	Orphans share only what they want you to know.
Sons are secure and will receive correction.	Orphans become defensive when corrected. They see correction as rejection and blame others.
Sons start out awkwardly in spiritual things, but gradually mature in them.	Orphans will not step out to take chances because they fear failure.
Sons are hopeful and expectant of the future.	Orphans would rather focus on the past.
Sons are more concerned about relationships.	Orphans are concerned about rules and regulations.
Sons have a stake in the family business, knowing they have an inheritance.	Orphans look for sundown and a pay check.
Sons stay put under fire.	Orphans look for greener pastures.

Modern business model versus a culture of sonship. We discovered that our staff, volunteer leaders, and elders were functioning in a business model not found in the New Testament. When the church lost momentum or difficult decisions were required, cracks appeared and exposed the weaknesses of the business model versus a culture of sonship.

Leadership in the New Testament Church was founded on honor and sonship. Sonship is seen in the relationship between Jesus and His Heavenly Father. Jesus submitted to the will and guidance of the Father in all things (John 5:19). He did not see himself as equal to the Father and took the place of a servant, being obedient to death (Philippians 2:6-8).

"Spiritual umbrella". God places, in every church, spiritual fathers and mothers with the authority to hold a "spiritual umbrella". Under this umbrella, the work of God flourishes, people are united, and the enemy has no authority to divide. The "umbrella person" is a first among equals, appointed by God to be servant-hearted and to love others with the heart of the Heavenly Father. We need to know who holds the umbrella, and honor and respect their leadership.

Additional Resources

In the "Extra Material" section at the end of the book, readers can download a copy of the *Southern Cross Centre Members Handbook*. Contained in the handbook are three articles that provide an expanded discussion of issues raised in this chapter:

- Building A Culture of Sonship

- Understanding Spiritual Authority in the Church

- Seven Relational Values

Lessons Learned
A Culture of Sonship

LEADERSHIP MODEL

In the church, the old leadership wineskin is based on a CEO and portfolio model. The new leadership wineskin is based on a culture of sonship.

QUALITIES OF LEADERS

Essential qualities in a church leader are integrity, loyalty to the senior leader, being a team player, and a good work ethic.

WAIT ON THE LORD

We make more mistakes by rushing into decisions rather than delaying them.

DEFINITION OF SONSHIP

A culture of sonship is a culture of honor. We honor others whenever we show respect and behave in a way that adds value to their lives.

GIFTS AND FRUIT

The gifts of the Spirit should always be held in equal balance with the fruit of the Spirit.

LEADERSHIP POSITIONS

Only spiritual sons or daughters should be appointed to leadership positions. Avoid placing any person with an orphan spirit in leadership.

SELECTING LEADERS

When selecting prospective leaders, we should look for four qualities: *character, competence, chemistry* and *calling*.

IDENTITY IN CHRIST

Knowing God's favor comes from understanding our identity in Christ. We must first become sons and daughters of God before we can become sons and daughters in the house.

ENEMY'S ATTACK

When a key leader falls, it gives the enemy permission to attack a church.

CHAPTER SIX: GOOD IDEAS OR GOD IDEAS?

I tell you the truth, the Son can do nothing by himself; he can do only what he sees his Father doing, because whatever the Father does the Son also does.

JOHN 5:19

Sometimes it seems easier to copy what someone else is doing than to wait on the Lord for fresh revelation. I pursued many good ideas that I discovered later were not God's ideas. For two decades, we tried to introduce ministry models that had been developed outside of Churchlands. In addition to the Bethel School of Supernatural Ministry, we introduced programs from Natural Church Development (NCD), Teamwork Bible College, Alpha, Willow Creek Community Church, and 3DM. I was shocked to discover I was merely repeating the same strategies and programs that had already been successful at Churchlands.

It is only by forgetting yourself that you draw near to God.

HENRY DAVID THOREAU

Thinking

A wise person once said, "It is insane to think that by doing the same things, in the same way, over and over, you will get a different result." I had always thought of myself as an innovative person, open to new ideas and new ways of doing things. It came as quite a shock when I discovered I was trying to repeat strategies based on previous moves of God at Churchlands.

Because I spent insufficient time waiting on the Lord for direction, I ended up repeating newer versions of past programs. They may have worked previously at Churchlands, but God was wanting to move us into a new apostolic direction. What I assumed were good ideas were not actually 'God ideas.'

The Lord used four things to shift my thinking in His direction:

1) The changing spiritual landscape of our city.

2) Planting two Bible Training Schools.

3) The growth of Churchlands Community Services.

4) My involvement with the Australian Coalition of Apostolic Leaders.

The Changing Landscape of Perth

God used rapid societal changes to catch my attention. In the new millennium, overseas immigration to Perth increased. This changed the religious demographic of our city in two ways: 1) non-Christian religions started to grow, and 2) many new churches were planted across the city.

The introduction of new religions, while inevitable, convoluted a widely held belief that Australia was a nation founded on Judeo-Christian principles. The growth of world religions resulted in a strong push for multi-culturalism and a growing sentiment that there was nothing particularly special or unique about Christianity. Jesus was increasingly seen as just one of 'many ways up the mountain'.

Unfortunately, planting new churches, while also inevitable, had an unanticipated result. Big churches seemed to get bigger and small churches were increasingly struggling to survive. At a time when planting new churches was mooted as the best way to evangelise Australia, I saw just the opposite. The overall number of Christians was not increasing but church attenders now had more choices.

Some churches grew by catering to distinct cultural and ethnic groups. Others targeted a particular demographic, e.g., youth, young families, and young adults. I struggled with the competitive spirit emerging from these new 'attractional' churches. Christian unity often hangs by a slender thread of goodwill and trust among pastors. Goodwill was diminishing but nobody seemed to care.

About this time, an international leader who pioneered 'seeker sensitive' churches began visiting Perth regularly. He was an impressive communicator. Soon pastors across the city were repeating a mantra that churches become more "culturally relevant".

This seemed very wrong. The Kingdom of God is counter-cultural. God's Word stands in contradiction to the worldly philosophies of relativism, individualism, hedonism, and consumerism. What I saw developing in Perth was not growing God's Kingdom. I heard many good ideas, but few God ideas.

During this season, Churchlands continued to host conferences, albeit with decreasing numbers. We hoped that hosting cutting edge speakers like Francis Frangipane, Bill Johnson, Graham Cooke, Brother Yun, Greg Burson, Steve Sampson, Rick Joyner, Jack Deere, John Chacha, Rita Johnson, and Alan Meyer would equip the saints to embrace the Kingdom of God.

We could see that the spiritual atmosphere of Perth was changing. This caused us to amp up our emphasis on prayer. For fifteen years, Churchlands hosted monthly city-wide prayer breakfasts. Every

Thursday, Ron Ings, my associate pastor, and I would drive across the city to pray in various churches. As the years passed, we began to feel discouraged, like our prayers were hitting a glass ceiling. Were we praying outside of God's purposes? What was the Father doing that we seemed to be missing?

Bible Training Schools

God revealed the importance of waiting on Him through two unsuccessful attempts to establish Bible training schools.

Our first attempt, in 2004, was when I was persuaded to establish a Churchlands campus of Teamwork Bible College. Teamwork was founded by Dr John Chacha and had been very successful in Africa. After the first semester, it became clear that the Teamwork teaching material was not suited to the Australian culture. The school was then disbanded.

In 2011, we decided to establish the Churchlands School of Supernatural Ministry (CSSM). In March 2010, Bill Johnson, pastor of Bethel Church in Redding, California, spoke at Churchlands on "Bringing Heaven to Earth". Bethel had already established a successful School of Supernatural Ministry.

Again, I was persuaded that Schools of Supernatural Ministry were operating successfully in Australia. I hoped the school would bring back the power evangelism and signs and wonders we had experienced at John Wimber's conferences in the 80s and 90s.

To establish the school, we invited a team of former Aussie Bethel students. CSSM grew quickly and attracted over two hundred students from across the Perth metropolitan area. Unfortunately, the school's somewhat radical approach to supernatural ministry polarized Churchlands, much to my surprise. Half of the congregation enrolled in the school and loved it. The other half were turned off by what they felt was excessive behavior.

Soon after the school began, it became apparent that those I had appointed to lead CSSM had their own ideas about how the school should operate. The School of Supernatural Ministry had begun to operate as an entity separate to the church. The hopes we had for CSSM were never realized.

While teaching was excellent and practical, CSSM closed after two and a half years when it failed to attract new students. Once CSSM closed its doors, few students or teachers remained as part of the Churchlands community.

Lessons Learned from Bible Training Schools

So, what did we learn from our experience with Teamwork and CSSM?

1) ***A good idea is not always a God idea.*** While starting a school of ministry based on outside models seemed like a good idea, it was not a God idea.

2) ***Challenges of transplanting ministry.*** It is difficult to transplant a ministry model that works in one place into an entirely different sphere.

3) ***Challenges of importing people.*** The best leaders in a church are those who have proven to be spiritual sons and daughters in the house. It is unwise to import outside people, regardless of how gifted they may seem, to lead a ministry.

4) ***Follow the Lord's template.*** The best way to equip the saints is to follow a template revealed by the Lord and led by local church leaders.

Churchlands Community Services (CCS)

The history of Churchlands Community Services can be traced back to our move to 154 Balcatta Road in 1991. It was originally established to assist struggling families and individuals in need of food or clothing.

We had the good idea that meeting people's practical needs would provide evangelistic opportunities to lead them to Christ. While CCS became an effective outreach ministry to the community, we fell short in the task of evangelism.

Churchlands Community Services involved many gifted men and women whose hard work enabled the ministry to thrive. The relationship between Churchlands Christian Fellowship and CCS was symbiotic. The church provided facilities and material support, while CCS regularly served meals for church events and became an important avenue for church members to participate in hands-on ministry.

For over twenty years, CCS Community Café offered weekly free meals and basic foodstuffs. Each Wednesday, the café included spiritual input and entertainment from a variety of speakers, musicians, and community groups. In the latter years of CCS, Alpha was also introduced.

CCS is a good example of good ideas versus God ideas. What started out as a God idea slowly morphed, changed, and grew into an entity that had its own vision and purpose. Ministry to the poor and needy, while an important aspect of loving others, can become the main focus of a church and distract people from other God-directed priorities.

Lessons Learned from CCS

We learned a few lessons from our experience with CCS:

1) **Eating together.** Eating together is a catalyst to Christian fellowship. Relationships are built through the eating and sharing of food, as we see in the church in Jerusalem in Acts 2:42, "They devoted themselves to the apostles' teaching, and to the fellowship, to the breaking of bread and to prayer."

2) **Limited success.** Relatively few food recipients became

involved in the wider life or ministry of Churchlands. For many, CCS became a church within a church. This was not healthy.

3) **Shifting focus.** CCS became mistaken by several members as the major focus and purpose of Churchlands' ministry. This was never our intent. Community service and feeding the poor are acts of service that build bridges and alleviate poverty. The primary purpose of the church is to be the community of the Kingdom, to worship God, and make and deploy disciples to advance the Kingdom across society.

4) **Fostering a culture of entitlement.** Giving away food can foster a culture of entitlement and dependence rather than generosity.

5) **Dependency on pastors.** Some CCS activities maintained a chaplaincy and pastoral culture, dependent on the ministry and leadership of pastors.

The Australian Coalition of Apostolic Leaders (ACAL)

Sometimes what appears to be a good idea turns out to be a God idea. In early 2015, Alaine and I were approached to become national convenors of the Australian Coalition of Apostolic Leaders. We did not seek this position but were approached and asked if we would take it on. We knew ACAL was heading toward decline, so we said yes.

While we did not have absolute confirmation from God, saying yes has been one of the best decisions we have ever made. During our five years as national convenors, our horizons expanded. My confidence grew as I learned to engage with an eclectic mix of strong and talented leaders.

During our five years as national convenors, ACAL was shaped into a cohesive group for advancing Apostolic Reformation in Australia. We pioneered four initiatives:

1) The ACAL National Council was established, a working group of key apostolic leaders in each of the six Australian states. The Council met regularly to coordinate ACAL activities in Queensland, New South Wales, Victoria, Tasmania, South Australia, and Western Australia.

2) The ACAL Members Booklet. This resource defined the coalition and its history, vision, strategy, and priorities.

3) The annual ACAL National Summit was expanded into a two-day, three-night event, rotating between the states of NSW, QLD, TAS, SA, and VIC.

4) ACAL hosted national speaking tours of two key international apostolic leaders: John Kelly, International Convenor of International Coalition of Apostolic Leaders (ICAL) and Joseph Mattera, National Leader of United States Coalition of Apostolic Leaders (USCAL).

Involvement in ACAL has influenced my understanding of apostolic reformation, key apostolic priorities, the current state of the church, and the priority of building apostolically-configured churches.

The timing of our involvement came at a crucial moment when we were transitioning from Churchlands to Southern Cross Centre. What started as simply stepping in to fill a gap, turned out to be God's plan positioning us to establish a prototype.

Institutional Lifecycle

The following bell-curve illustrates the institutional lifecycle of a church.

Churches go through multiple stages during their existence. The lifecycle starts with "Infancy" that signifies the birth of a church. Church growth takes a church from "Childhood" into "Adolescence" until it reaches full "Maturity". The church then experiences a drop in energy and find itself at a T-junction. It either continues declining and enters an "Old Age" and "Death", or escapes "Death" with a reset by the Holy Spirit that takes the church into a new lifecycle.

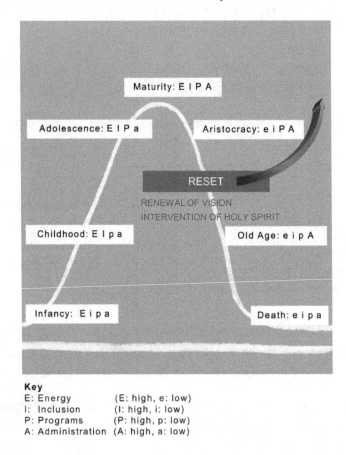

Key
E: Energy   (E: high, e: low)
I: Inclusion   (I: high, i: low)
P: Programs   (P: high, p: low)
A: Administration   (A: high, a: low)

Graph 1 Institutional Lifecycle

There are four dynamics that indicate where a church is positioned on the institutional lifecycle. These four dynamics are:

1) *Energy*—the level of enthusiasm and volunteerism in a congregation.

2) *Inclusion*—the ability of a church to attract and include new

people.

3) *Programs*—the activities and opportunities a church offers for spiritual growth, service, or the wellbeing of its people.

4) *Administration*—the team who lead or coordinate the work of the church.

Energy is a form of momentum. John Maxwell, in *21 Irrefutable Laws of Leadership*, highlights a leadership principle he calls the "Big Mo". The "Big Mo" is momentum. As long as your organization has momentum, all is well. Once momentum begins to wane, it affects the inclusion of new people and places additional pressure on the leadership team.

In churches, inclusion comes through conversion or transference, by people coming to faith in Christ, or by transferring from another church. When people are enthusiastic about their church, they talk about it and invite others to join them.

Two foundational programs in churches are cells and celebration, i.e., small groups and worship services. Programs can be age-orientated or need-specific: ministry to children, youth, adults, and seniors, counselling, social assistance, and outreach to the community.

Administration refers to paid or volunteer leaders who oversee the work of the church. They can be professional, managerial, administrative, technical, or can be caretakers. Administration normally refers to staff who oversee, plan, and evaluate the programs, facilities, and running of the church.

Energy and inclusion create the need for more programs and administration. After a church reaches maturity, energy and inclusion diminish, the church moves toward aristocracy and old age.

It is possible to reverse decline and reset a congregation as the Holy Spirit intervenes to birth a new work (see "Reset" between "Aristocracy" and "Old Age" in Graph 1). This happened at Churchlands Christian Fellowship when the move from 154 Balcatta Road led to the birth of Southern Cross Centre.

CONCLUSION

Institutional lifecycle. Churchlands' institutional lifecycle lasted thirty-two years before a significant event from the Holy Spirit transformed it into Southern Cross Centre. For eleven years, from 1987 to 1998, Churchlands progressed from infancy to maturity. From 1998 to 2008, Churchlands plateaued and began the decline into aristocracy. In 2008, the Holy Spirit spoke through Graham Cooke when he brought a powerful prophetic word to Churchlands. What followed was an eleven-year period of pruning, from 2009 to 2019, until the sale of the church building at 154 Balcatta Road led to establishing Southern Cross Centre.

Pain for our good. As a leader, I inadvertently attempted to repeat past moves of the Spirit by pursuing good ideas instead of God ideas. Some of my choices brought painful consequences. Pain drew me closer to God and taught me to wait on Him.

Holy Spirit-led. Experience has taught me God's ways are above my ways. I came to see that my soul (my mind, will and emotions), was guiding many of my decisions. God wanted me to be more Spirit-led and bring my soul under the guidance of His Holy Spirit.

Promise and hope. As I reflected on our thirty-two-year journey at Churchlands, I felt led to meditate on Haggai 2:9, "'The glory of this present house will be greater than the glory of the former house,' says the Lord Almighty. 'And in this place, I will grant peace,' declares the Lord Almighty."

I paused and asked, *Lord, what could be greater than the glory of Churchlands? Churchlands was awesome! We saw your manifest presence and goodness! What could be greater than the glory of the former house? The Lord impressed on me the words of Watchman Nee,*

The tide of the Spirit is a rising tide, never stationary but always moving forward.

On my ministry journey (in "Part One" and "Part Two"), I now see that God was teaching me lessons that would shape the blueprint of an apostolically-configured church. In Part Three, we begin by examining the priorities and practices of Jesus and the apostles as seen in the Kingdom of God and the dynamics of three New Testament churches. This provides a foundation for understanding ten current apostolic priorities. We will then explore how these priorities are embodied in Southern Cross Centre.

Lessons Learned — GOOD IDEAS OR GOD IDEAS?

APOSTOLIC REFORMATION

Apostolic reformation is defined as, "returning God's people to the priorities and practices of Jesus and the Apostles".

REVIVAL VS. REFORMATION

Revivals are powerful but short-lived moves of the Spirit. The church needs more than revival, it needs reformation.

PROTOTYPE

The prototype God wanted to establish in Perth was a church that was apostolically-configured.

EQUIPPING THE SAINTS

Schools of ministry are insufficient in equipping the saints for the work of ministry and shaping mature disciples. We must explore life in the New Testament church to discover new models for equipping.

INSTITUTIONAL LIFECYCLE

All congregations go through the institutional lifecycle. Each stage is necessary and has lessons that teach important insights.

REDEMPTIVE PURPOSES

When God allows things to be shaken, His purposes are always redemptive.

GUIDANCE

As leaders, we must pursue the Holy Spirit to guide our thinking and strategies.

DISTRACTION

Successful programs can become a distraction from the main purposes of the church.

MOMENTUM

Momentum is your friend. As long as an organization has momentum, all is well. Once momentum begins to wane, problems come to the surface.

ACCELERATION

When we see what the Father is doing and cooperate with Him, things take less time.

PART THREE: THE PROTOTYPE

CHAPTER SEVEN: THE SECRET KINGDOM

The vision has its own appointed hour, it ripens, it will flower; if it be long, then wait, for it is sure, and it will not be late.

HABAKKUK 2:3 (Moffatt Translation)

Jesus' primary message during His earthly ministry was the Good News of the Kingdom of God. The Kingdom is the summation of Jesus' priorities and practices. God's Kingdom points to His government over all things in heaven and earth. We can enter and inhabit God's Kingdom only by the power of the Holy Spirit. The evidence of our habitation is righteousness, peace, and joy in the Holy Spirit. The Kingdom is already present in part but is yet to be seen in its fullness. When Jesus returns, God's Kingdom will be established in its fullness. Until then, we see it only in part and are tasked with advancing God's rule by discipling nations.

For no one can lay any foundation other than the one already laid, which is Jesus Christ. If any man builds on this foundation using gold, costly stones, wood, hay or straw, his work will be shown for what it is, because the Day will bring it to light. It will be revealed with fire, and fire will test the quality of each man's work.

I CORINTHIANS 3: 11-13

The Good News

The Kingdom of God is largely secret and invisible to the naked eye. We cannot see or enter the Kingdom of God except through faith and doing what we perceive God is telling us to do. When we trust God and act on His Word, incredible power is released to change outcomes and fulfil God's will on earth.

The Kingdom of God, more than any other reality, reveals the priorities and practices of Jesus Christ. His message was that we can live under the governance of God in this earthly life as a foretaste of life in eternity. Life in God's Kingdom is a Spirit-empowered existence that results in righteousness, peace, and joy in the Holy Spirit.

The Kingdom is a Treasure

Jesus came to reveal the true nature of God and the pathway to the Father. The Kingdom is the pathway God has set to obtain eternal life. We must enter God's Kingdom on earth to be assured of everlasting life in eternity.

The goal of every Christian is to become more like Jesus. No amount of knowledge, piety, or human effort will make us more like Jesus. We need the power of the Holy Spirit. The Spirit changes us from the inside out by increasing God's grace in us.

In 2 Peter 1:3-4 we read, "His divine power has given us everything we need for life and godliness through our knowledge of him who called us by his own glory and goodness. Through these he has given us his very great and precious promises, so that through them you may participate in the divine nature and escape the corruption in the world caused by evil desires."

God's Kingdom is the greatest goal to which any human being can aspire. Those who pursue the Kingdom receive blessings beyond measure. Jesus said in Matthew 6:33, "Seek first his kingdom and his righteousness and all these things will be given you as well." The

Kingdom and righteousness are inextricably bound. The Kingdom is the government of God, and righteousness is the nature of God. When we are filled with the Holy Spirit, we increasingly reflect the nature of God and expand His government throughout the earth.

The Kingdom is inhabited by sons and daughters of God. In Romans 8:14, we see that those who are led by the Spirit of God are his sons. As God's sons, we obey Jesus' great commission to disciple nations, and His government in the earth increases.

As nations are discipled and taught to obey Jesus' commandments, righteousness and justice will be established in the earth. This will shift the spiritual atmosphere and weaken the enemy's grip over creation.

This is why Romans 8:19 says, "all of creation waits in eager expectation for the sons of God to be revealed." When we advance the Kingdom, we return the earth to God's original plan for creation.

The Gospel of the Kingdom is a treasure because it will hasten Christ's second coming. Jesus will not return until the Gospel of the Kingdom is preached across the earth. Matthew 24:14 confirms that "this gospel of the kingdom will be preached in the whole world as a testimony to all nations, and then the end will come."

Peter taught it is possible to speed the day of Jesus' return, 2 Peter 3:11-12, "live holy and godly lives as you look forward to the day of God and speed its coming." When we advance God's Kingdom and cooperate with His plans, it results in an acceleration of time and history.

In summary, the Kingdom is a treasure because: 1) it gives assurance that we will inherit eternal life, 2) it is the key to a blessed life, 3) it returns the earth to God's original purposes before the fall, 4) it shifts the spiritual atmosphere of earth, and 5) it will hasten the second coming of Christ.

Entering and Inhabiting the Kingdom

Kingdom comes from the Greek word *basilea*, which means "the realm in which a sovereign king rules". Jesus announced that He is the gate, the portal, to living in relationship with the Heavenly Father and to receiving citizenship in His Kingdom.

John 1:12-13, "Yet to all who received Him, who believed on His name, he gave the right to become children of God—children born not of natural descent, nor of human decision or a husband's will, but born of God."

Jesus' discourse with Nicodemus in John 3:1-16 reveals our entry point to the Kingdom of God. In John 3:5-6, Jesus said, "I tell you the truth, no one can enter the kingdom of God unless he is born of water and the Spirit. Flesh gives birth to flesh, but the Spirit gives birth to (our) spirit." To enter the Kingdom of God we must be born of water and of the Spirit. This means we must be born again, baptised in water, and filled with the Holy Spirit.

How do we know when we are living in God's Kingdom? Paul answers this in Romans 14:17, "For the kingdom of God is not a matter of eating and drinking, but of righteousness, peace and joy in the Holy Spirit." When our lives evidence righteousness, peace, and joy it indicates we are living in God's kingdom.

Paul's intent was to warn believers not to be concerned about trivial matters like eating and drinking and miss the essence of Christian living. Only by grace given by the Holy Spirit can we live consistently righteous lives. Living in righteousness brings peace and joy.

Human beings are triune in nature. This means we consist of three parts: body, soul, and spirit. Prior to knowing Christ, we are guided primarily by the soul (mind, will, emotions). The goal of the Christian life is to become led by the Spirit. This happens when God's Holy Spirit inhabits our human spirit, which in turn, directs the attitudes and decisions of our soul. To enter and remain in God's Kingdom requires that we live in a manner directed and empowered by the Holy Spirit.

While the Holy Spirit inhabits our human spirit when we are born again, we need to be constantly re-filled with the Holy Spirit. This requires us to keep on knocking, asking, and seeking the Lord for top-ups of the Spirit's power.

Failure to be re-filled with the Spirit, opens us to spiritual attack in the form of discouragement, distractions, and deception. These, in turn, compromise our capacity to remain firmly under God's rulership, guidance and protection in His Kingdom. The key to remaining in the Kingdom depends on the ongoing empowering of the Spirit working in our lives.

In Romans 8:1-17, Paul explains how to live in the power of the Holy Spirit. To live in the Spirit requires that our minds are focused on what the Spirit desires (v. 5). The Spirit guided mind is no longer controlled by our inherently sinful nature (v. 9). The Spirit enables us to put to death the misdeeds of the Body (v. 13). In James 4:6, we see that God gives us grace when we humbly position ourselves before God. Grace is the desire and power to do God's will.

God is the one who enables us to live righteous lives. When we daily humble ourselves and ask God to re-fill us with His Spirit, He gives us grace to live in righteousness as citizens in His Kingdom.

Two signs that we are citizens of the Kingdom are the presence of peace, the tranquil countenance flowing from a clear conscience, and joy, the overflow of happiness that comes from knowing we have pleased God.

Difference Between the Gospel of the Kingdom and Salvation

Some in the church have mistakenly interpreted the Gospel of the Kingdom to be the Good News of Salvation. Salvation by grace through faith in Jesus is the essential doorway into the Kingdom of God. Living in the Kingdom, however, is much more involved. Righteousness in the

Holy Spirit compels us to advance God's government in the earth. Those who inhabit the Kingdom show the fruit of repentance. They are committed to discipling nations and teaching them to obey all that Jesus commanded.

The Gospel of the Kingdom includes salvation but is not limited to it. Salvation is only the beginning. God's purpose was to create a multigenerational army who could continue Jesus' ministry on earth until He returns. God wants His people to permeate and influence all of creation with the Good News that in this life we can live under God's rule.

Those who limit the Gospel to preaching salvation do not fully understand the Kingdom of God. Jesus never intended for His disciples to be gathered and corralled in buildings. He wants us to be ambassadors of His Kingdom, sent into every sphere of society, to be the salt and light of the earth.

The Church is Not the Kingdom

One reason for writing this book is my perception that few church attendees understand or actually enter the Kingdom of God. The Kingdom remains for them like an undiscovered treasure laying buried in a field. Many believers mistakenly think the church is the Kingdom, or that by joining a church God automatically places them in His Kingdom. Both views are incorrect.

The church is the community of the Kingdom, not the Kingdom itself. Theologian George Eldon Ladd wrote in *A Theology of the New Testament* (p. 109):

> "The Kingdom is primarily the dynamic reign or kingly rule of God, and, derivatively, the sphere in which the rule is experienced. In biblical idiom, the sphere is not identified with its subjects. They are the people of God's rule who enter it, live under it, and are governed by it. The church is the community of the Kingdom but never the Kingdom

itself. Jesus' disciples belong to the Kingdom as the Kingdom belongs to them; but they are not the Kingdom. The Kingdom is the rule of God; the church is a society of women and men."

As Ladd points out, the church is not the Kingdom, it is the community of the Kingdom. God's Kingdom is embodied in the church to the extent that His rule is practiced within it. In my experience, this has not always been the case. To be the community of the Kingdom requires that we live together in the righteousness, peace, and joy that emanates from the Holy Spirit's presence in us.

Narrow is the Gate

Jesus came to reveal the pathway to eternal life. Faith in Him is the gate into the Kingdom. We must enter the Kingdom during our earthly lives in order to be assured of life with God in eternity.

In Matthew 7:13-14 Jesus said, "Enter through the narrow gate. For wide is the gate and broad is the road that leads to destruction, and many enter through it. But small is the gate and narrow the road that leads to life, and only a few find it." Living in the Kingdom is the narrow road that leads to eternal life.

When Jesus said to his disciples, "The Kingdom of God is within you," He was speaking of the condition of our hearts. The heart is what motivates our thoughts and actions. The Kingdom is within us to the extent that Jesus rules our lives and behavior. Only the Holy Spirit can generate the desire and power to do the will of God. This is why we must be born of the Spirit to enter the Kingdom (John 3:5).

To be filled with the Spirit is to be filled with God's grace. Grace is the Holy Spirit produced desire and power to do God's will. The process of God's grace is explained in Philippians 2:12-13, "Continue to work out your salvation with fear and trembling, for it is God who works in you to will and to act according to his good purpose."

Here, the words fear and trembling can be confusing. Some Christian groups teach that salvation is only a one-time event. I have discovered salvation involves the process of becoming more like Jesus. This process takes a lifetime. Seen in this way, we work out our salvation, not with anxiety, but with reverence for God and responding to His grace. God's grace works in us to act according to His purposes.

Small is the gate and narrow is the path that leads to life; only a few find it. Jesus was speaking here, not to unbelievers, but to believers. Many church attenders have not yet found the righteousness, peace, and joy in the Holy Spirit that indicates we are living in God's Kingdom. For this, I am partly to blame, as are many pastors, for not preaching the Gospel of the Kingdom.

The Kingdom of God is built one person at a time. Churches can no longer afford to be silent or vague about the Gospel of the Kingdom. To do so is to threaten the eternal destiny of every believer.

We must heed Jesus' warning in Luke 13:23-27, "Someone asked him (Jesus), "Lord, are only a few people going to be saved?" He said to them, "Make every effort to enter through the narrow door, because many, I tell you, will try to enter and will not be able to. Once the owner of the house gets up and closes the door, you will stand outside knocking and pleading, 'Sir, open the door for us.' But he will answer, 'I don't know you or where you come from.' Then you will say, 'We ate and drank with you, and you taught in our streets.' But he will reply, 'I don't know you or where you come from. Away from me, all you evildoers!'"

Jesus is the gate and God's Kingdom is the path that leads to eternal life and few find it. Pastors are the spiritual gatekeepers of churches and cities. Now is the time to hear and heed Jesus' words in Mark 1:15, "The time has come...The kingdom of God is near. Repent and believe the good news!"

Kingdom Reconciliation

Jesus had a ministry of reconciliation. This makes the Kingdom of God a place of reconciliation. Paul clarified the importance of our ministry of reconciliation in 2 Corinthians 5:17-19, "Therefore, if anyone is in Christ, he is a new creation; the old has gone, the new has come! All this is from God, who reconciled us to himself through Christ and gave us the ministry of reconciliation; that God was reconciling the world to himself in Christ, not counting men's sins against them. And he has committed to us the message of reconciliation."

Today, as Christians, it is so easy to judge the world, and keep our distance from those whose sins are obvious or who flagrantly ignore God and His precepts. In Matthew 24:12-13, Jesus warned His disciples, alluding to the days prior to His second coming, "Because of the increase of wickedness, the love of most will grow cold, but he who stands firm to the end will be saved."

As evil gets worse, we must continually guard our hearts against the stronghold of 'cold love'. We must never give up on loving the lost and those who have strayed. Love hopes all things, believes all things, and endures all things. We must never stop loving others, regardless of what they may have done or their lifestyle.

The Greek word for sin is *hamartia*, an archery term meaning to "miss the target" or "miss the mark". Sin is any attitude or behavior that deviates from, or is less than, how God created us to live. We have all missed the mark at some time.

Jesus taught that there is only one sin that cannot be forgiven, blasphemy against the Holy Spirit. Therefore, any other sin can and should be forgiven by us. The reason we must forgive is that without forgiveness, we cannot be reconciled to God or to each other.

While sin can and should be forgiven, to knowingly persist in a sinful lifestyle will keep us from entering the Kingdom. We read in 1 Corinthians 6:9-10, "Do you not know that the wicked will not inherit the kingdom of God? Do not be deceived. Neither the sexually immoral nor idolators nor adulterers nor male prostitutes nor homosexual offenders not thieves nor the greedy nor drunkards nor slanders nor swindlers will inherit the kingdom of God."

To live in the Kingdom is much broader than being part of the church, it is loving others as God loves them. The Greek word for 'love' is *agape*. *Agape* is unconquerable benevolence. We display *agape* when we look at another person and say, "What can I do to help you become the greatest of who you can be in Christ?" In 1 John 4:16b we read, "God is love. Whoever lives in love lives in God, and God in him." To live in the Kingdom is to live life by loving as God does.

Twelve Principles (Laws) of the Kingdom

The Kingdom of God functions according to a series of principles that we find in the teachings of Jesus. Each principle reveals an aspect of how the Kingdom works. When the principles are applied, God's power is released to bring about His purposes. Pat Roberson in his book, *The Secret Kingdom*, highlights eight of the principles. To these, I have added four.

1) The Principle of Forgiveness

Luke 6:37, "Do not judge, and you will not be judged. Do not condemn and you will not be condemned. Forgive and you will be forgiven." Jesus revealed the Father's heart when He forgave sins. If we want to be forgiven of our sins, we must first learn to forgive others. Forgiveness aligns us with God and releases His power to work in every situation. In the Kingdom, mercy triumphs over judgment.

2) The Principle of Honor

Matthew 10:41, "Anyone who receives a prophet because he is a prophet will receive a prophet's reward, and anyone who receives a righteous man because he is a righteous man will receive a righteous man's reward." Whenever we recognize and embrace grace, a gift of

God, in another person it pleases God. It positions us to give them the honor they deserve and to receive what God wants to impart to us through them.

3) The Principle of Greatness

Mark 10:43, "Whoever wants to be great among you must be your servant, and whoever wants to be first must be a slave of all." This principle teaches that the greatest in the Kingdom is the one who serves. Authority in God's Kingdom manifests itself, not in ambition or self-promotion, but from selfless acts of love. God promotes those who lay down their lives by loving others above themselves.

4) The Principle of Perseverance

Matthew 7:7 "Ask and it will be given you; seek and you will find; knock and the door will be opened to you. For everyone who asks receives; he who seeks finds; and to him who knocks the door will be opened." This principle teaches that, in God's Kingdom, good things come to those who persevere. Perseverance is essential to develop hope in us (Romans 5:3-4). It shapes in us the truth of Romans 8:28, that "in all things, God works for the good of those who love God and are called according to His purposes."

5) The Principle of Sowing and Reaping (Reciprocity)

Luke 6:38, "Give and it will be given to you. A good measure pressed down shaken together and running over will be poured into your lap. For with the measure you use, it will be measured to you." This principle teaches that we reap what we sow. In God's Kingdom, those who sow generously, reap generously. God sees all and rewards those who sow generously (finances, kindness, love, forgiveness, etc.).

6) The Principle of Responsibility

Luke 12:48 "From everyone who has been given much, much will be demanded, and from the one who has been entrusted with much, much more will be asked." This principle teaches that greater position and authority in the Kingdom brings increased responsibility and accountability. We see this in James 3:1, "We who teach will be judged more strictly." and Hebrews 13:17, "Obey your leaders and submit to their authority. They keep watch over you as men who must give an account."

7)   The Principle of Use

Matthew 25:29, "For everyone who has will be given more, and he will have an abundance. Whoever does not have, even what he has will be taken from him." The Principle of Use says use it or lose it. If we do not invest what God has given us, He will take it away and give it to someone who will. The path to promotion in God's Kingdom is to be faithful in small tasks.

8)   The Principle of Miracles

In Matthew 21:21-22, Jesus said, "I tell you the truth, if you have faith and do not doubt, not only can you do what was done to the fig tree, but you can also say to this mountain, 'Go, throw yourself into the sea,' and it will be done. If you believe, you will receive whatever you ask for in prayer." Miracles occur when God suspends natural laws to bring about a different result. God is the author of miracles, but He also uses human beings as conduits of His power. Miracles occur through a process: 1) the Holy Spirit speaks to our spirit about what God wants to do, 2) our spirit speaks to our mind, 3) our mouth speaks, or we physically act on what the Spirit is doing, and 4) the miracle occurs. Unforgiveness impedes the flow of God's power. We must make sure there is no unforgiveness in our hearts.

9)   The Principle of Unity

Matthew 18:19-20, "Again, I tell you that if two of you on earth agree about anything you ask for, it will be done for you by my Father in heaven. For where two or three come together in my name, there I am with them." This principle is based on the perfect unity found in the Holy Trinity (Father, Son and Holy Spirit). Unity results when people hear from God, agree upon what they have heard, and combine efforts to accomplish what God has said. Unity results in synergy.

10) The Principle of Dominion (Stewardship of the Earth)

Genesis 1:28, "God blessed them (Adam and Eve) and said to them, 'Be fruitful and increase in number; fill the earth and subdue it. Rule over the fish of the sea and the birds of the air and over every living creature that moves on the ground." God wants His children to recapture the dominion mankind held at the beginning of creation. Dominion does not mean domination; it means to steward creation and fulfill the purposes for creation as God intended. Mankind's dominion in the earth was forfeited by sin, to Satan and his minions. To restore man's dominion over creation, the Father sent His Son, the second Adam, to restore what was lost in Eden.

11) The Principle of Binding and Loosing

Matthew 16:19, "I will give you the keys of the Kingdom of Heaven; whatever you bind on earth will be bound in heaven, and whatever you loose on earth will be loosed in heaven." Jesus gave His disciples authority to open spiritual doors or close them. Whatever we permit (loose) will be permitted and whatever we oppose (bind) will be stopped. The Greek tense of the words, 'binding' and 'loosing', implies that "it has already been bound or loosed in heaven". This implies that our permissions or sanctions should always reflect God's will.

12) The Principle of Spiritual Battle

Matthew 11:12, "From the days of John the Baptist until now, the kingdom of heaven has been forcefully advancing, and forceful men lay hold of it." The Kingdom of God is advanced by courageous and forceful men and women. When we enter the Kingdom, we become aware of the spiritual battle raging around us. The Kingdom is no place for avoiding conflict or remaining uncommitted. Advancing God's Kingdom requires courage, vigour, power, and persistence because of ever-present opposition.

Two Parables of the Kingdom

Jesus taught His disciples about the Kingdom of God by using parables. Parables are illustrations from everyday life that give insights into the workings of God's Kingdom. Luke 8:10, "The knowledge of the secrets of the kingdom of God has been given to you, but to others I speak in parables, so that, 'though seeing, they may not see; though hearing, they may not understand.'" Jesus wanted His disciples to understand the "secrets" of the Kingdom, but those who lacked faith or had evil motives would be confounded by His parables. We give two parables as examples.

I.   The Parable of the Sower (Matthew 13:3-9, 18-23)

"Then He told them many things in parables, saying: 'A farmer went out to sow his seed. As he was scattering seed, some fell along the path, and birds came and ate it up. Some fell on rocky places, where it did not have much soil. It sprang up quickly, because the soil was shallow. But when the sun came up, the plants were scorched, and they withered because they had no root. Other seed fell among thorns, which grew up and choked the plants. Still other seed fell on good soil, where it produced a crop—a hundred, sixty or thirty times what was sown.'" (Matthew 13:3-9).

"'Listen then to what the parable of the sower means: When anyone hears the message about the kingdom and does not understand it, the evil one comes and snatches away what was sown in his heart. This is

 the seed sown along the path. The one who received the seed that fell on rocky places is the man who hears the word and received it at once with joy. But since he has no root, he lasts only a short time. When trouble or persecution comes because of the word, he quickly falls away. The one who received the seed that fell among the thorns is the man who hears the word, but the worries of this life and the deceitfulness of wealth choke it, making it

unfruitful. But the one who received the seed that fell on good soil is the man who hears the word and understands it. He produces a crop, yielding a hundred, sixty, or thirty times what was sown.'" (Matthew 13:18-23).

~The Meaning of the Parable of the Sower~

This parable speaks of four ways people respond to the word of God. Jesus was preparing His disciples for the kind of responses they would get when proclaiming the gospel.

The first person has a hard heart. They hear the word but don't believe it because they are *deceived*—the enemy snatches the word from them.

The second person is open to the word but when trouble or persecution comes, they quickly fall away. They are easily *discouraged*.

The third person is *distracted* by worldly worries and wealth and looks for fulfillment in lesser realities. Deception, discouragement, and distraction are the main reasons people hear the gospel yet fail to become fruitful disciples of Jesus.

The fourth person hears the word and understands it. He does not merely hear the Word, he responds, comes into fellowship with other believers, grows to maturity, and produces a lifelong harvest of good fruit in the Kingdom of God.

Kingdom insights from the parable. This parable helps us understand why the path to eternal life is narrow, and why few find it. Only one person out of the four who heard the word actually bore fruit. It alerts us to the enemy's tactics to derail our walk with God. Deception, distractions, and discouragement are the primary reasons people resist the gospel or fall away. The parable exhorts believers to persevere and stay focused in our walk with God. Only the test of time reveals those who produce a harvest, like the seed that fell into good soil.

II.   The Parable of the Weeds (Matthew 13:24-30, 36-43)

"Jesus told them another parable, 'The kingdom of heaven is like a man who sowed good seed in his field. But while everyone was sleeping, his enemy sowed weeds among the wheat, and went away. When the weeds sprouted and formed heads, the weeds also appeared.

The owner's servants came to him and said, 'Sir, didn't you sow good seed in your field? Where then did the weeds come from?'

'An enemy did this', he replied. The servants asked him, 'Do you want us to go and pull them up?'

'No,' he answered, 'because while you are pulling the weeds, you may root up the wheat with them. Let both grow together until the harvest. At that time, I will tell the harvesters: First collect the weeds and tie them in bundles to be burned; then gather the wheat and bring it into my barn.'" (Matthew 13:24-30).

"Then he left the crowd and went into the house. His disciples came to him and said, 'Explain to us the parable of the weeds in the field.' He answered, 'The one who sowed the good seed is the Son of Man. The  field is the world, and the good seed stands for the sons of the kingdom. The weeds are the sons of the evil one, and the enemy who sows them is the devil. The harvest is the end of the age, and the harvesters are angels. As the weeds are pulled up and burned in the fire, so it will be at the end of the age. The Son of Man will send out his angels, and they will weed out of his kingdom everything that causes sin and all who do evil. They will throw them all into the fiery furnace, where there will be weeping and gnashing of teeth. Then the righteous will shine like the sun in the kingdom of their Father. He who has ears, let him hear.'" Matthew 13:36-43).

~The Meaning of the Parable of the Weeds~

Jesus used this parable to explain the origins of evil in a world that God had created for good. He then shifted to an allegorical interpretation of the story: Jesus is the sower of the good seed, the field is the world, and the good seeds are the sons of the Kingdom. The weeds are the sons of the evil one, and the enemy who sowed the bad seed is Satan. The harvest is the end of the age and the harvesters are angels, who will gather in the end time harvest.

At the end of the age, Christ's second coming, the sons of evil will be gathered and sentenced to judgement, where there will be great remorse and suffering. The sons of the Kingdom will also be gathered. They will shine with righteousness in the Kingdom of their Father.

God purposed that good and evil will grow side by side until the harvest. The sons of light and sons of darkness will increase until the second coming of Jesus. This explains why murder, violence, wars, and mayhem are increasing, while at the same time, there are more men and women who are Christians now than at any point in history.

Kingdom insights from the parable. Good and evil grow side by side, not only in the world, but in the church as well. We note Jesus called the good seed, "sons of the kingdom". These sons are wise and will lead many to righteousness. This fulfils the end time prophecy found in Daniel 12:3.

The church is currently poised for a reset. Covid-19 has brought churches to a T-junction. We can choose to function as we have in the past, or we can embrace the Kingdom of God. When churches focus on making disciples who enter the Kingdom, "sons of the kingdom" will be released in the earth, and many will be led to righteousness.

Jesus also warned of wolves who would come and mercilessly savage the flock of God. These are the weeds that grow among the wheat. They gather to themselves the unwary, the spiritually immature, and those seduced by the world's pleasures. Because of the lure of these false and immature church leaders, countless naïve and well-intentioned believers will fall prey to their apostasy, abuse, and ambition.

CONCLUSION

The Gospel of the Kingdom was Jesus' primary message during His earthly ministry. To understand the Kingdom of God is to know the priorities and practices of Jesus. Jesus is the King in the Kingdom of God. When we obey Jesus' commandments and put them into practice, we place ourselves under the governance of God.

We have examined several aspects of the Kingdom of God:

- ♛ Why it is a treasure

- ♛ Entering and Inhabiting the Kingdom

- ♛ Differences between the Gospel of the Kingdom and Salvation

- ♛ Differences between the Church and the Kingdom

- ♛ The Narrow Gate into the Kingdom

- ♛ Kingdom Reconciliation

- ♛ Twelve Principles (Laws) of the Kingdom

- ♛ The Parables of the Kingdom

In the following chapter, we turn to the priorities and practices of the apostles as we reflect on life in three New Testament Churches and the missionary journeys of Paul.

CHAPTER EIGHT: A TALE OF THREE CHURCHES

They devoted themselves to the apostles' teaching and to the fellowship, to the breaking of bread and to prayer...And the Lord added to their number daily those who were being saved.

ACTS 2:42, 47b

Now that we better understand the Kingdom of God, we turn to the priorities and practices of the apostles. The apostles were the architects of the early Church. In the Book of Acts, we discover three churches that model what it means to be 'apostolically-configured'. Jerusalem, the mother church, is a model of Biblical community. Ephesus, a major Asian city located at the crossroad of two major trade routes, hosted an evangelistic equipping centre. Antioch, a key seaport in the eastern Mediterranean, became a church that deployed evangelists to spread the Kingdom message into the Roman Empire.

History is the "track of God's footsteps through time." It is in His dealings with our forefathers that we may expect to find the laws by which He will deal with us.

CHARLES KINGSLEY

Priorities and Practices of the Early Apostles

We have chosen the Churches at Jerusalem, Ephesus, and Antioch to give an insight into the priorities and practices of the early apostles. Our task is to discover the characteristics of these churches that are timeless and relevant in our day. The first Christian churches were named according to the city or area where they were located. Believers often met in small home gatherings and only occasionally in larger groups.

Early churches were established by apostles who would then appoint elders. These elders were trained by the apostles and became part of a team to oversee the local church. Apostles usually only had spiritual authority over churches they had planted. An exception to this may have been the original twelve apostles of Jesus, who had greater authority because they had been eyewitnesses of Jesus' ministry.

The word 'church' appears in the New Testament thirty-five times. The Greek word for church, *ekklesia,* means "a calling out". In the original Jewish sense, *ekklesia* was a popular meeting, a religious congregation, synagogue, Christian community, or assembly.

The Church at Jerusalem: Community and Oneness

Jerusalem is known as the "holy city". To the Jew and the Christian, Jerusalem is a city set apart by God. Venerated by the Jews as Mount Zion, Jerusalem was the site of three Jewish temples.

In Roman times, the city was a centre of government and commerce. Jerusalem was where Jesus ministered, was crucified, resurrected, and the Holy Spirit given to the early church. Jerusalem is the birthplace of Christianity. It is where the first believers had met and begun to spread the message of Christ across the earth.

Before ascending to heaven, Jesus said to his disciples, "'Do not leave Jerusalem, but wait for the gift my Father promised, which you have heard me speak about. For John baptised with water, but in a few days, you will be baptised with the Holy Spirit...you will receive power when the Holy Spirit comes on you; and you will be my witnesses in Jerusalem, and in all Judea and Samaria, and to the ends of the earth.'" (Acts 1:4-5, 8).

Holding onto Jesus' words, the apostles remained in Jerusalem. At the Feast of Pentecost, fifty days after Passover, a hundred and twenty God-fearing Jews from every nation gathered in an upper room in the city to pray. They received the gift of the Holy Spirit and began to speak in tongues.

Following the Pentecost outpouring of the Spirit, many foreign Jews decided to remain in Jerusalem. Far from home, they would have needed food and lodging. The believers at Jerusalem stepped up to meet these needs. As they gathered for teaching, fellowship, food, and prayer, the early believers shared with each other and gave to those in need.

The Church at Jerusalem grew quickly after Peter's bold speech in Acts 2. Three thousand believers were added to their number in one day. Persecution, threats, and accusations from Jewish religious authorities did little to deter the original believers. In Acts 5:42, we read, "Day after day, in the temple courts and from house to house, they never stopped teaching and proclaiming the good news that Jesus Christ is Lord."

Two Scriptures reveal what life was like in the Jerusalem Church:

Acts 2:42-44, "They devoted themselves to the apostles' teaching and to the fellowship, to the breaking of bread and to prayer. Everyone was filled with awe, and many wonders and miraculous signs were done by the apostles. All the believers were together and had everything in common."

Acts 4:32, "All the believers were one in heart and mind. No one claimed that any of his possessions was his own, but they shared everything they had."

The Jerusalem church was a model of true Christian community. There are several dynamics present in the Jerusalem church that can be applied to modern churches: sharing the Good News of Christ, teaching, prayer, generosity, freedom in the Spirit, and oneness. The Jerusalem church was filled with people who loved God and loved each other.

Lessons from Jerusalem

ONENESS

There was unity, oneness of heart and mind.

HOLY SPIRIT POWER

The power of the Holy Spirit was tangible as people prayed and ministered to each other.

GENUITY

Genuine, beneficial, and loving relationships.

GENEROSITY

Believers shared what they had. They were generous. They also distributed food to those in need.

ORGANIC MEETINGS

Their meetings were not limited to the Sabbath but could happen at any time. Meetings were not limited to large gatherings but were often informal, going from house to house.

KEY INGREDIENT

Small gatherings included four things: teaching, fellowship, food, and prayer.

BOLDNESS

Teaching and proclaiming that Jesus is Lord was done boldly and by all.

The Transition from Disciple to Apostle

At Jerusalem, early church leaders were trained, and functioned in challenging circumstances. Acts 8 reveals that Christians were persecuted and all except the apostles were scattered from Jerusalem. In Acts 15, we see that the apostles and elders who remained in Jerusalem formed an apostolic council. The city was eventually destroyed by the Romans in 70 AD.

Jesus originally called His twelve followers "disciples", from the Greek *mathetes*, meaning "one who learns". Apostle comes from the Greek word, *apostolos*, meaning "one who is sent". In Matthew 10:1-4, we observe the twelve disciples were commissioned as apostles before they were sent out as part of their training by Jesus.

Being sent out to the neighboring communities was a preparation for what was to come. In Acts 1:8, before His ascension to heaven, Jesus told the twelve, "'But you will receive power when the Holy Spirit comes on you; and you will be my witnesses in Jerusalem, in all Judea and Samaria, and to the ends of the earth.' "When the Holy Spirit came upon them at Pentecost, the twelve disciples took up an ambassadorial role of becoming Christ's witnesses to advance the Kingdom of God.

The transition from disciple to apostle provides an important insight into Jesus' plan for spreading the gospel and planting churches. It was never Jesus' intent that the apostolic role would cease with the original twelve apostles. Being sent was to become a major activity in the New Testament church and remains important in the church today.

Apostles in the New Testament were not limited to the original twelve disciples of Jesus. The New Testament records that James, the half-brother of Jesus and leader of the Jerusalem church, was an apostle (James 1:19). Other apostles in the New Testament are Barnabas (Acts 14:14), Apollos (4:6-9), Timothy and Silvanus (I Thessalonians 1:1 and 2:6), Epaphroditus (Philippians 2:25), two unnamed apostles (2 Corinthians 8:23), and Andronicus and Junia (Romans 16:7). The most well-known of all these apostles was Paul of Tarsus, who became an apostle to the Gentiles and wrote much of the content of the New Testament.

Paul's Missionary Journeys

Although most of my ministry has focused on pastoring in a local church, I have travelled extensively to unfamiliar places to minister to the Body of Christ. This has given me an appreciation of the strategic and tactical ways Paul the Apostle carried out his missionary activities to the Gentiles.

Paul had begun by being part of a small team with no more than one or two missionary companions. Next, he had progressed to taking small teams along with him. Finally, he discovered the value of spending extended periods of time in strategic cities, Corinth, Ephesus, Rome, and multiplied his effectiveness by being a resident equipper.

On Paul's first missionary journey, he travelled with Barnabas and John Mark around the eastern fringe of the Mediterranean. They went first to Cyprus, which had been home to Barnabas. It was the custom of Paul and Barnabas to preach first at the synagogue to the Jews, and then reach out to Gentiles.

Next, they travelled north to the area of Galatia and to Pisidian Antioch, Iconium, Lystra, Derbe, Pisidia, Pamphylia, and Perga. The Word of the Lord spread through the entire region. New churches were established, and elders were appointed to oversee them. They continued the same pattern of preaching, teaching, and winning new converts before returning to Antioch.

On the second missionary journey, Paul travelled with Silas and revisited the churches he had previously established. Paul's plan was to leave a strong local Christian community in each place he visited. Later, he would either revisit these communities or keep in contact through letters. In Lystra, Paul invited Timothy to join the team on their journey. Feeling forbidden by the Spirit to enter Asia, the team ended up in Troas. In Troas, Paul had a vision of a man in Macedonia pleading for help. Thus, began the evangelization of Europe.

In Europe, Paul and Silas ministered in Phillipi, Thessalonica, Berea, Athens, and Corinth, where he met Priscilla and Aquila, who continued with him as far as Ephesus. Paul's aim was to establish strong Christian communities in the major cities of the Roman Empire. He spent much of his second journey in Corinth. By the time he left Corinth, the church had become a strong and a well-organized community. After a brief stop in Ephesus, Paul travelled to Jerusalem and reported to the apostles. He then returned to Antioch.

On his third journey, Paul travelled first to Ephesus. After the Jews rejected his message, he left the synagogue and took the believers with him. In Ephesus, Paul hired facilities at the school of Tyrannus and established a school for evangelization and equipping. He taught Jews and Greeks, from the surrounding province of Asia, the message of "the Way", and about the Kingdom of God (Acts 19:10).

The impact of Paul's sojourn in Ephesus was profound. Many of his students were sent out to establish churches in the surrounding region. As the Church in the city grew, the spiritual atmosphere of Ephesus began to change. New converts burned their occult books. The pagan cult and economic system surrounding the Temple of Artemis were thrown into chaos by the increasing influence of Christians.

When Paul left Ephesus, he travelled to Troas and Miletus before returning to Jerusalem. In Jerusalem, Paul was put on trial and sent as a prisoner to Rome, where he was eventually martyred.

Lessons from Paul's Ministry

We discover important priorities and practices Paul developed to expand the Kingdom:

Strategic importance. Paul selected cities of strategic importance to spread the Gospel message, some examples are: Ephesus, Athens, Pisidian Antioch, Philippi, Corinth, and Thessalonica. In many cities, Paul suffered violent opposition. In the two places where he was not expelled, Corinth and Ephesus, Paul stayed for an extended time and had great influence.

Taking advantage of inroads. Paul was also tactical in his thinking. When he visited a city, he went first to the synagogue to take advantage of the custom that would allow a stranger to address the gathering. He also met many non-Jews at synagogues. This gave him inroads to reach an entire city.

Ministry of the Word and Holy Spirit. Paul emphasized the ministry of both the Word and the Spirit. He was well grounded in the Scriptures and moved powerfully in the gifts of the Holy Spirit.

Personal encounters. Paul's major impact came, not solely from preaching at large meetings, but as a result of personal and small group encounters. Paul was highly relational. This gave him considerable influence in the lives of those he ministered to.

Establishing churches. Paul was a master builder when it came to church planting.

- He targeted strategic cities and established churches that were organized, self-sustaining, self-perpetuating, and able to advance the Kingdom of God.

- He trained and selected elders to lead the churches. These elders were indigenous and mature believers, spiritual sons who were accountable to the apostles.

- He continued to supervise and keep contact with the churches he founded. The elders would oversee the churches in Paul's absence. He kept in touch by personal visits, sending one of his protégés to visit in his stead, and writing letters of instruction.

Plying his trade. Paul made allowance for the financial support of his ministry by plying his trade of making tents. He avoided placing financial burdens on his converts and churches.

Raising up apprentices. Paul raised up apprentices to assist him and carry on his work. He left a legacy by passing on his baton of faith and leadership to many spiritual sons.

The Church at Ephesus: A Culture of Equipping

Ephesus was the most important city in Asia Minor, now Turkey. Located at the intersection of two major trade routes, Ephesus was a commercial centre. It boasted a pagan temple dedicated to the Roman goddess Diana, the Greek equivalent being Artemis. The temple of Diana was one of the seven wonders of the ancient world.

Paul made Ephesus a centre for evangelism and equipping. He spent more time in Ephesus than any other city during his missionary journeys. On his third journey, after his message was rejected in the synagogue, Paul continued with daily Kingdom teaching in the lecture hall of Tyrannus, a local philosopher or rhetorician.

We read of this in Acts 19:10-11, "This (teaching) went on for two years, so that all the Jews and Greeks who lived in the province of Asia heard the word of the Lord. God did extraordinary miracles through Paul, so that even handkerchiefs and aprons that touched him were taken to the sick, and their illnesses were cured, and the evil spirits left them."

Paul equipped his students both by teaching and demonstrating God's power. "My message and preaching were not with wise and persuasive words, but with a demonstration of the Spirit's power." (1 Corinthians 2:4).

He also emphasized the importance of leaders who can reproduce themselves, "And the things you have heard me say in the presence of many witnesses entrust to reliable men who will also be qualified to teach others." (2 Timothy 2:2). Paul's ministry at Ephesus greatly multiplied the number of church leaders in Asia Minor.

The church in Ephesus became the New Testament model of an equipping community. Paul's discussion on five-fold equippers in Ephesians 4:11-13 indicates that apostles, prophets, evangelists, pastors, and teachers played a key role in the equipping centres in Ephesus, and possibly in Antioch, in Pisidia (Acts 13:14), Thessalonica (Acts 17:11), Athens (Acts 17:15), and Corinth (Acts 18:1).

The Five-fold Ministry

In Ephesians 4, Paul explains the model Christ established for equipping the saints. When Jesus ascended to heaven, He divided His ministry giftings into five parts, which He then distributed to all believers. However, some believers were given a greater portion of His gifting, so they could prepare God's people for works of service.

Ephesians 4:7, 11-13, "But to each one of us grace has been given as Christ apportioned it...It was he who gave some to be apostles, some to be prophets, some to be evangelists, some to be pastors and teachers, to prepare God's people for works of service, so that the Body of Christ may be built up, until we all reach unity in the faith and in the Son of God, and become mature, attaining to the whole measure of the fullness of Christ."

During Jesus' earthly ministry, He perfectly modelled each of the five-fold ministry gifts. He was the supreme apostle, the most gifted prophet, the most effective evangelist, He taught as one with authority, and was the "good shepherd". The fruit of His ministry is seen in His twelve disciples, who became apostles and continued Jesus' work on earth.

It is important to note Ephesians 4:7, "to each one is given". This verse implies that every believer has received a measure of Christ's power to do ministry. Jesus determines how much of His anointing each believer receives. Every believer has some measure of the ministry gifting of apostle, prophet, evangelist, pastor, or teacher. While the New Testament is not specific on this subject, I have observed four levels of grace in believers.

Four Levels of Grace

To understand these four levels of gifting for ministry, we use the prophetic gift as an example:

- *Level One*—Occasional expression of the gift. The person gives occasional, general, non-specific, prophetic words that bring encouragement or comfort.

- *Level Two*—Regular expression of the gift. The person becomes aware of their gifting and starts to be recognized as having a prophetic gift. As they exercise the prophetic gift, the words they give become more accurate and produce good fruit. At this point, the person's gifting is noticed and, ideally, someone at level three or four begins to mentor them.

- *Level Three*—Ministry. The person is recognized as having a mature prophetic ministry. They are persons with gifting and character, mature in Christ, bearing good fruit, and are submitted to their leaders.

- *Level Four*—An Equipper. This person has all the qualities of Level Three plus a demonstrated ability to equip and release others into effective ministry. They are disciples who make disciples.

Equippers, at the fourth level of gifting, should evidence both anointing (ministry gifting) and spiritual authority. Spiritual authority, *exousia*, is God's permission to give spiritual leadership and significantly advance His Kingdom. Those having spiritual authority can be recognized by the significant degree of revelation, wisdom, humility, and fruit of the Spirit they evidence.

I have observed that relatively few believers ever reach level three or four. Why? First, because Christ alone determines the amount of grace a believer will receive. Ministry grace is a gift from God, not something we can master through study or experience. The second reason is that few believers can persevere in the tests and trials required to develop the character required of a five-fold equipper.

Restoration of the Five-fold Ministry

The five-fold ministry are not merely trainers and equippers within the Body of Christ; they are men and women who have persevered and paid a high price to follow Jesus. Led by the Spirit, they evidence the anointing and authority of Christ. They are totally committed to advancing the Kingdom of God on earth.

I believe the function of apostles, prophets, evangelists, pastors, and teachers has continued in each generation since the days of the early church. Only recently, however, have the five ministries come back to the radar screen of the church as essential for preparing God's people for works of service.

Ultimately, only God can restore the five-fold ministry to the Church. Jesus is the one who distributes His grace as He sees fit. However, I am beginning to see a pattern in how the five-fold grows. Jesus begins with apostles and prophets working together (see Ephesians 2:20). Together, the apostle and prophet carry a synergistic gifting that lays foundations for the other five-fold ministries, such as evangelist, teacher, and pastor, to emerge.

God's people will come to reflect the fulness and maturity of Christ only to the extent that the five-fold ministry gifts function in a local church or geographical region. We must therefore consider restoring the five-fold ministry as a top priority.

Pursuing Afresh

In spite of its great strengths, the church in Ephesus eventually declined to the point of receiving a rebuke from the Holy Spirit in Revelation 2:4-5, "Yet I hold this against you: You have forsaken your first love. Remember the height from which you have fallen! Repent and do the things you did at first. If you do not repent, I will come to you and remove your lampstand from its place."

It is estimated that this rebuke was written twenty to thirty years after Paul lived and ministered in Ephesus. Each generation must pursue the purposes of God afresh and not become complacent in the Lord's work. The tide of the Spirit is always a rising tide, never stagnant or receding. To keep step with the Spirit we must actively pursue God and remain committed to advancing His Kingdom.

Lessons from Ephesus

CHURCH'S MISSION

Define your church's mission in terms of building community, equipping, and deployment. Consider how to establish an equipping centre as Paul did at the school of Tyrannus.

ESTABLISH ELDERSHIP

Establish an eldership as the form of church oversight. Elders should fulfil the qualifications set out in 1 Timothy 3:1-7. They should also be in relationship to and accountable to an apostle who is linked relationally to the church.

WORD AND SPIRIT

Emphasize the importance of the Word and Holy Spirit. Be well grounded in the full counsel of God's Word. Embrace and welcome the ministry of the Spirit.

PLAN FOR EQUIPPING

Develop a plan for equipping the saints that includes both teaching and hands on experience.

RAISE UP FIVE-FOLD

Raise up and acknowledge the five-fold ministry graces according to the four levels of gifting.

RECOGNIZE EQUIPPERS

Recognize five-fold ministry equippers in the local church or region and allow them to minister according to the grace they carry. All true equippers carry both anointing and spiritual authority.

CHURCH CULTURE

Establish a culture of sonship and honor in the local church. Spiritual sons and daughters gradually grow into spiritual fathers and mothers. Do not place anyone into a position of leadership unless they are a spiritual son or daughter in the house.

STAY ARMED

Be prepared for spiritual warfare and opposition when you begin to configure a church apostolically.

The Church in Antioch: A Sending Community

Antioch was an important seaport on the east coast of the Mediterranean. Two cities are named Antioch in the Book of Acts. One is in Syria and the other in Pisidia in Asia Minor. The story of the church in Syrian Antioch is found in three places: Acts 11:19-20, Acts 13:1-3, and Acts 14:21-28.

Following severe persecution directed at the Church in Jerusalem, many Jewish believers fled to Syrian Antioch. In their new home, they shared the Good News with the Greeks, a number of whom turned to the Lord. When news of this development at Antioch reached Jerusalem, Barnabas was sent to encourage the new believers. In need of assistance, Barnabas went to Tarsus to look for Saul and bring him to Antioch.

Together, Barnabas and Saul strengthened the church leaders and taught great numbers of people. It was in Antioch that followers of Jesus were first called "Christians".

Eventually, Saul and Barnabas were deputised by the church and sent to Jerusalem. On their return to Antioch, several church leaders, including prophets and teachers, were led by the Spirit to release Saul and Barnabas on what is now known as Paul's First Missionary Journey. Saul, who was soon to be renamed Paul, used Antioch as his base for his three missionary journeys.

Lessons from Antioch

STRATEGIC AND TACTICAL

The mission focus of the church at Antioch was both strategic and tactical. Strategic thinkers develop plans and strategies for expanding the Kingdom. Tactical thinkers develop tactics to break strongholds and overcome opposition to the Gospel.

PROGRESSIVE STRATEGY

Paul's missionary journeys from Antioch illustrate a progressive strategy in spreading the Gospel. First, Paul travelled with one or two individuals. Next, he travelled with a team. At Corinth, he began to see the value of church planting that involved living for an extended period in a city. Finally, Paul developed an apostolic equipping centre in a strategic regional centre at Ephesus.

MISSIONARY BASE

Antioch was a church committed to Kingdom expansion. We can surmise that Paul used Antioch as his base for missionary work because many believers supported his work.

PROPHETS AND TEACHERS

In Antioch, we see prophets and teachers working together to equip the saints. This speaks of the importance of the Word and Holy Spirit being combined to mature believers. Paul's ministry reflected this balance of the Word and Spirit.

THREE FOUNDATIONAL AREAS

At Antioch, the church was strong in three foundational areas: community, equipping, and deploying. These three emphases are crucial in an apostolically-configured church.

INDIGENOUS LEADERS

Antioch, as a cultural melting pot, would have reinforced Paul's focus of raising up indigenous leaders to lead new works.

Antioch is the model of a New Testament church committed to sending missionaries to advance God's Kingdom. Many believers in Antioch had experienced persecution and diaspora. This caused Antioch to develop a stronger focus on sending evangelists than what was seen in the church at Jerusalem.

CONCLUSION

A closer look at the strategies of Paul in his three missionary journeys, combined with life in three New Testament churches in Jerusalem, Ephesus, and Antioch, reveal key priorities and practices of the early apostles. The churches reveal that community, equipping, and deploying are three characteristics of an apostolically-configured church.

Jerusalem. Jerusalem provides us with a model of Biblical community. The church at Jerusalem points us to community based on apostolic teaching, fellowship, breaking bread together and prayer. Generosity and kindness are foundational to establishing relationships of love and trust. Loving God and loving one another transforms churches into communities of the Kingdom.

Ephesus. The church at Ephesus became a centre for equipping and evangelism. Paul made Ephesus his home for over two years. During this time, he trained and deployed many believers to establish churches in the surrounding region of Asia Minor. We can surmise that all five equipping ministries in Ephesians 4 were present in the Church at Ephesus. In Ephesus, as God's Kingdom advanced, the spiritual atmosphere of the city shifted noticeably.

Antioch. The seaport city of Antioch was used as a base by the Apostle Paul for his three missionary journeys to the Gentiles. The Antioch Church was committed to training and sending workers into the harvest field. Antioch became a strategic location for launching ships that carried evangelists to spread the Gospel across the Roman Empire.

Our study of the Kingdom of God and the early church provide us with keys to understanding apostolic foundations. In the next chapter, we examine ten apostolic priorities that will assist churches to reconfigure their focus.

CHAPTER NINE: BUILDING ON APOSTOLIC FOUNDATIONS

Therefore, everyone who hears these words of mine and puts them into practice is like a wise man who built his house on the rock. The rain came down, the streams rose, and the winds blew and beat against that house; yet it did not fall.

MATTHEW 7:24-25

Our goal is to establish a modern prototype of an apostolically-configured church. From our study of the priorities and practices of Jesus and the apostles, we discover three pillars of an apostolic church: 1) Kingdom focus, 2) the ministry of the Word and Spirit, and 3) churches that focus on building community, equipping, and sending. In this chapter, we set forth ten priorities that will help re-configure today's churches to a more apostolic direction.

The foundations of our society and our government rest so much on the teachings of the Bible that it would be difficult to support them if faith in these teachings should cease to be practically universal in our country.

CALVIN COOLIDGE

Understanding the Prototype

In 2008, Graham Cooke announced at Churchlands that Perth was going to see a "new prototype" of church, I began asking, *What is a prototype?* 'Prototype' is defined as "a first or preliminary version of a device or vehicle from which other forms are developed"[1]. Every prototype is made up of two components, the frame or design of the vehicle and the cargo or components it contains.

When Jesus announced the formation of His Church, He was announcing a prototype. Up to that point, no one was aware that Jesus was about to establish an entirely new vehicle for fulfilling God's purposes. Jesus first spoke of this vehicle, the church, at Caesarea Phillipi, on Peter's confession of Him as the long-awaited Christ, the son of the living God:

Matthew 16:17-19, "Jesus replied, blessed are you, Simon son of Jonah, for this was not revealed to you by man, but by my Father in heaven. And I tell you that you are Peter, and on this rock, I will build my church, and the gates of Hades will not overcome it. I will give you the keys of the kingdom of heaven; whatever you bind on earth will be bound in heaven, and whatever you loose on earth will be loosed in heaven."

The Greek word for church, *ecclesia,* means "those who are called out". By using this word, Jesus painted a picture that would have been understood by His hearers. The *ecclesia* were the "elders of a city" who sat at the city gate and determined who and what would be permitted to enter their area of jurisdiction. This explains why Jesus spoke of the keys to the Kingdom in the context of binding and loosing, permitting, and forbidding.

Binding and loosing needs some clarification. Jesus was not saying the Church would have authority to bind and loose everything at their

---

[1] Oxford English Dictionary

discretion. The Greek tense used in the terms 'binding' and 'loosing' means "have already been bound in heaven" or "have already been loosed in heaven". What Jesus meant was the Church can only bind or loose in accordance with the Father's will.

Occasionally, church leaders sanction practices that are not in line with God's Word. This is why churches must return to the teachings of the Scripture to guide what we should approve of and what we should forbid. When the church sanctions practices that are contrary to God's Word, the result is moral confusion, lawlessness, and division.

Foundation of Jesus Christ

When it comes to building, foundations are essential. Paul wrote in 1 Corinthians 3:10-11, "By the grace God has given me, I laid a foundation as an expert builder, and someone else is building on it. But each one should be careful how he builds. For no one can lay any foundation other than the one already laid, which is Jesus Christ." We must return the Church to its true foundation by following the words, works and ways of Jesus.

Jesus is the only foundation in God's Kingdom. My experience is that churches often pay lip service to building on the foundation of Jesus. It is easy to fall back on familiar traditions or good ideas, instead of God ideas. A discussion of the four realms of authority will help clarify what Jesus expects of His Church.

Four Realms of Authority

God is the author of all authority. In the earth, He has established authority in four realms: the family, the Church, government, and voluntary associations (companies, businesses, clubs, special interest groups, etc.). Each of these four areas has clear boundaries and responsibilities.

The family is responsible for the raising, guidance, and nurture of children to adulthood. The church is responsible for expanding the rule of God on the earth and being the moral conscience of a nation. The government is responsible for passing laws that are just, provide for law and order, and reflect the immutable laws of God. Voluntary associations exist to provide fair remuneration and work conditions, and strengthen the social and economic wellbeing of a nation.

Society functions properly when each of the four realms operate wisely and remain in their proper jurisdiction. Problems arise when one realm of authority imposes its power on the authority of another realm, e.g., when government legislates to curb the authority of the church or family, or conversely, when the church tries to manipulate the government.

Many problems in modern society stem from the Church retreating from the world, rather than engage with it. The Church is responsible for expanding God's rule and the knowledge of His Commandments. It is called to disciple entire nations, not just to make individual disciples.

The Church also has responsibility to strengthen families by building into parents who, in turn, nurture children in the knowledge of the ways of God. Increasingly, the responsibilities of parents are being overshadowed by governments, through schools and education. The results are often horrific.

God's plan is to return His Church to its original realm of authority. Our first step is to configure the church properly on its biblical foundations. The following ten priorities will guide us in building on proper biblical and apostolic foundations.

Ten Apostolic Priorities

1) Understanding and learning to live in our identity as New Covenant believers.

Churches need to instruct people in how to embrace and live in our New Covenant identity. We need to understand and live out what it means to be a new creation in Christ. Knowing our identity in Christ is a prerequisite to exercising our authority as children of God.

    2)   Training believers to embrace a biblical, versus an atheistic or humanistic, worldview.

Our worldview is the lens through which we see the world and define what is true. Our worldview shapes our values and behaviour. The prevalent modern worldview is often at loggerheads with what the Bible teaches. Embracing a non-biblical worldview inhibits us from living under God's rule and entering His Kingdom.

The Body of Christ must no longer be silent or intimidated from expressing beliefs based on the biblical worldview. We must learn how to counter and expose humanistic and atheistic worldviews that oppose the knowledge of God. 1 Corinthians 10:5, "We demolish arguments and every pretension that sets itself up against the knowledge of God, and we take every thought captive and make it obedient to Christ."

    3)   Building true biblical community on the Book of Acts pattern.

The Church is the community of the Kingdom. We need to follow the example of the New Testament Church at Jerusalem. The Book of Acts (Acts 2:42-47, 4:32-35, and 5:12-16) reveals how the Jerusalem church built a strong sense of community. Our goal should be to establish fellowship with each other on the basis of apostolic teaching, fellowship, breaking bread, and prayer.

    4)   Restoring a culture of sonship and honor.

Strong churches are built on a culture of sonship. We need to build relationships that honor God and each other. Honor is based on gratitude and recognizing those who have added value to our lives. When we recognize and embrace God's grace in another person, it positions us to give them the honor they deserve, and to receive what God wants to impart to us through them.

    5)   Turning the hearts of spiritual and biological fathers and

mothers toward the children.

In an apostolically-configured church, spiritual fathers and mothers pass their baton of faith to the next generation of believers. To become a spiritual mother or father, we must first be a spiritual son or daughter. Cultures of sonship and honor are essential to developing intergenerational relationships that leave a spiritual legacy.

6) Restoring the function of the five-fold equipping ministries of Ephesians 4:11-13.

As we have seen, when Jesus ascended to heaven, He divided His ministry into five functions which He then distributed, as gifts through the Holy Spirit, to all believers. Some of these believers have been chosen by God to be equippers of the saints.

God's people will reflect the fulness and maturity of Christ only to the extent that the five-fold ministry gifts function in a local church or geographical region. To re-establish the five-fold, we must:

- Understand and define the functions of the five anointings of apostle, prophet, evangelist, pastor, and teacher.

- Establish five-fold teams in churches and regions. This means recognizing five-fold equippers and potential equippers and developing a mentoring process.

- Equip the saints regardless of their stage of growth in their five-fold gifting. Develop a process of instruction, mentoring and deployment appropriate to each of the five functions.

- Understand the four-level process of growing in the five-fold to help people assess their level of development and develop in their ministry gifting.

7) Train believers to minister in the supernatural power of God.

All believers should be equipped to minister, not only with wise and persuasive words, but with demonstrations of the Spirit's power. This requires instructing and activating believers to minister in the gifts of the Holy Spirit. Ministry in the Spirit should give a particular focus to evangelism and healing in the power of the Holy Spirit (see John Wimber and Kevin Springer books *Power Evangelism* and *Power Healing*).

The power of the Holy Spirit demonstrates how God's rule breaks into the present world. Living in the Kingdom requires us to become supernaturally natural. The supernatural power of God should be demonstrated through us in daily life.

8) Learning to make disciples who are mature and able to reproduce themselves.

Jesus followed a simple pattern in making disciples. He modelled something and His disciples observed Him, Then, the disciples repeated the action while Jesus watched and gave them feedback. Jesus then sent his disciples out and told them to do what they had been taught. They then reported back to Jesus. Finally, the disciples did what Jesus had taught them and taught others how to do it.

Jesus made disciples by living among the twelve. He took His disciples on a journey that included instruction, interaction, demonstration, activation, and deployment into the harvest field. The primary activity of an apostolically-configured church is to make disciples who will make other disciples. Jesus' model for making disciples is our model.

9) Sending and deploying believers into missional activity outside of the local church.

Jesus commissioned His disciples to be his "sent ones", witnesses to carry His message to the ends of the earth, and in doing so, to disciple entire nations. An apostolically-configured church equips men and women to infiltrate their sphere of influence and establish the values and practices of God's Kingdom.

The churches of Ephesus and Antioch equipped and sent workers into the harvest field. Every believer has a God-given ministry assignment. Believers should be assisted in discovering their assignment and be trained and sent to fulfil it.

10) Advancing the Kingdom of God in every realm of society.

Jesus told his disciples that the Kingdom of God is advancing by force, and forceful men are taking hold of it. The church's role is to raise up an army of men and women committed to advancing the governance of God throughout the earth.

Jesus prophesied that He would not return until the Gospel of the Kingdom had been preached as a testimony to every nation. A testimony is more than just words, it is words that have resulted in actions that transform the world around us. By advancing God's Kingdom in the earth, we continue the work of Jesus to reconcile the world to God, and bring all creation under His governance.

CONCLUSION

Priorities and practices of Jesus and the Apostles. The premise of this book is that the Church of Jesus Christ must return to its foundations in the New Testament. These foundations have been clarified through our study of the Kingdom of God, the missionary strategies of Paul, and the dynamics found in three key churches in the New Testament. From our study we are able to determine ten priorities that should be considered by modern churches that seek to be apostolically-configured.

Working models. From the priorities of an apostolically-configured church, we can develop prototypes and working models. These models are necessary for apostolic reformation to influence the mainstream (majority) of Christian thinking.

Innovation. The Diffusion of Innovation Curve Theory, developed by Everett M. Rogers in 1962, helps us understand that most leaders embrace new ideas only when they see working models of the idea in operation. Most current apostolic leaders now fall into the categories of innovators or early adopters. Below is a graph that illustrates the process of how new ideas are gradually accepted and implemented by the mainstream.

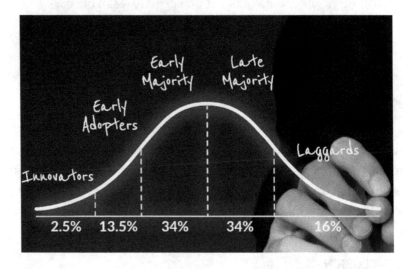

Graph 2 Diffusion of Innovation

The graph reveals that apostolic reformation is still in its early stages and embraced largely by "innovators" and "early adopters". To advance apostolic reformation to the next stage of "early majority", requires the development of prototypes and working models of apostolically-configured churches.

In the final chapter, we consider the way ahead by: 1) examining a model of an apostolically-configured church in process, Southern Cross Centre, and 2) conclusions I have reached from my journey in life and ministry.

CHAPTER TEN: THE WAY AHEAD

From the days of John the Baptist until now, the
kingdom of heaven has been forcefully advancing,
and forceful men lay hold of it.

MATTHEW 11:12

In the first six chapters, we examined highlights of my ministry journey in denominational, charismatic, and networking settings. I discovered that the churches I served in were incapable of being the light and salt Jesus has called His people to be. To address this problem, we are in the process of establishing Southern Cross Centre, a prototype of an apostolically-configured church. Most churches today are at a T-junction, deciding whether to continue with business as usual or to return to our New Testament roots, which includes Christ's ministry of reconciliation.

Nothing is stronger than an idea
whose time has come. There is one
thing stronger than all the armies in
the world, and that is an idea whose
time has come.

VICTOR HUGO

The Birth of Southern Cross Centre

The birth of Southern Cross Centre can be traced to events following the sale of the 154 Balcatta Road property in 2019. Only a remnant of the previous congregation remained as part of Churchlands after the building was sold. We met for two months on Sunday afternoons in our old building. Then, we leased a nearby community hall on Sundays. As we no longer had an office, we secured a small office suite in Balcatta.

Our seven remaining full and part-time staff began working in the newly rented facility. We needed to maintain basic services to help us begin to rebuild. This was a time of great uncertainty. Who would remain with us? What ministries would continue? Where would we ultimately re-locate? How would the new church be different?

I had peace in knowing God had asked Alaine and me to pioneer the new work. Where God guides, He provides. We began looking for a permanent place of worship. Perhaps we would relocate in a smaller factory building, an office complex, an old church, or a shopfront? We explored several properties, but none seemed suitable.

A real estate agent contacted us about an option that was on the horizon. A Jehovah's Witness Kingdom Hall in the nearby suburb of Balga would soon be up for sale. The building seated two hundred and forty, had ample parking, and was located in a residential area surrounded by lovely gardens. While the notion of this came as a surprise, I resolved to keep an open mind.

Balga had a reputation as one of Perth's less salubrious suburbs, but it was located near major freeways and was very accessible. My first view of the property was cautiously encouraging. The property had possibilities. Smaller and more welcoming than our factory building, the property was serene, with lovely trees and native plants, and large grassy areas. The building was tidy but a bit dated. As the property had previously been zoned as a church, we could begin services immediately.

After prayer, the elders and I organized a property valuation. Mindful of the asking price, we put in a sealed bid. We knew several other religious groups had shown interest in the property. Thankfully, our bid was accepted. The sale went quickly and smoothly. Within six months of leaving the Balcatta property, we were now the proud owners of a former Jehovah's Witnesses Kingdom Hall less than five kilometres from our previous location! I could not believe it!

There was a sense of relief when we announced news of the purchase. Then things began to accelerate. We formed a renovation team. We re-wrote our church constitution. Finally, we changed our name! At a congregational meeting in August 2019, we changed our name from Churchlands Christian Fellowship to Southern Cross Centre.

Vision for the New Church

During the previous months, I believe the Lord had been showing me some things about Southern Cross Centre:

A working model. The church was to become a prototype of a new genre of church that would provide a model of Christian churches in the future.

Modelled on Jerusalem, Ephesus, and Antioch churches. The new work would be modelled on three New Testament churches: Jerusalem, Ephesus, and Antioch. Its missional focus would be on building community, equipping, and deploying.

Apostolically-configured. The work would need to be apostolically-configured to reflect the priorities and practices of Jesus and the apostles.

Equipping centre. The church was to be an equipping centre for ministries in both the church and marketplace.

Vision and ethos of the Southern Cross Association of Churches. The church would reflect the vision and ethos of the Southern Cross

Association of Churches. This is why the name Southern Cross Centre was important.

Gathering place. Although located in a quiet suburban setting, the church would eventually be a gathering place for people nationally and internationally.

Resources on the journey. I needed to put my thoughts on paper to write the handbook and other resources that would help us on the journey of establishing a new Kingdom wineskin.

The SCC Members/Leaders' Handbook

We had not been in the new building very long when tensions arose in our leadership team. I could see that some were unclear about where the Lord was guiding us. A natural tendency is to go back to old ways of doing things. To counter this, I put together a manual for members and leaders. This booklet clarified several issues pertaining to our vision, priorities, and practices. The guide had two goals:

1) Present the standards and expectations we wanted to maintain among leaders at Southern Cross Centre.

2) Provide a reference for resolving conflict.

The booklet began with an historical overview of Southern Cross Centre. It then went on to clarify our vision, values, and ten apostolic mission priorities (discussed in "Chapter Nine").

The booklet then highlighted some key topics in an apostolically-configured church:

- Understanding our identity in Christ

- Building a culture of sonship

- Understanding spiritual authority in the church

- God's standard of financial giving

- Seven relational values (for resolving conflict)

- What it means to embrace the biblical worldview

- Ways to distinguish between the conviction of the Holy Spirit and the condemnation of the enemy

- Eleven stages in the development of disloyalty

The booklet has proven most helpful in clarifying our priorities, practices, and the church culture we are trying to establish. (A copy of the Handbook is available in the "Extra Material" section of this book).

The COVID-19 Pandemic

Following the release of the booklet, the world was hit by the rapid spread of the COVID-19 virus. This brought unprecedented changes in the way churches were permitted to operate. Gatherings of over ten people were no longer permitted and we had to find ways of connecting with our congregation online. Fortunately, we had a tech-savvy team to set up online broadcasting of our Sunday services. For three months, all church services were available only online.

Western Australia escaped the worst of the pandemic and widespread lockdowns. The pandemic was very destructive in other parts of Australia. The Australian Government was generous in allocating economic stimulus payments to businesses, including churches, to assist in paying salaries.

COVID-19 made it necessary for Southern Cross Centre to upgrade our media ministry. We purchased new video and production equipment to broadcast via internet to our members. This made it possible for Southern Cross Centre to equip and connect with the SCAC Network of ministries worldwide.

Our Strategy for the First Three Years

At Southern Cross Centre, we are in the process of implementing a strategy to transition us into a church that is apostolically-configured. Guided by the insights of G.T. Doran[2], we now focus on SMART goals that are specific, measurable, attainable, relevant, and time-based. Ten SMART goals for our first three years at Southern Cross Centre are:

   1)   Establish a house of prayer.

Our goals can be achieved only to the extent we have God's guidance, protection, and provision. Prayer at every level of leadership builds a foundation on which the work of God grows.

   2)   Follow Jesus' pattern for the sequential developing of leaders: the three, twelve, and seventy-two principle.

Jesus invested most of His effort into His inner circle of three disciples, Peter, James, and John, and the twelve original disciples. These twelve disciples lived and ministered with Jesus for three years. As time passed and the three and twelve became better trained, Jesus then included seventy-two more disciples to be trained and sent to spread the Gospel.

During the first two years, we will focus on training the "three" and "twelve". In the third year, we will select additional members, the "seventy-two", to be equipped for ministry and deployment.

   3)   Establish a Leadership Community (LC).

The leadership community is comprised of everyone in a church leadership capacity. Priority is given to training, equipping, and galvanizing the "three" (our staff and Elders) and the "twelve" (volunteer leaders of ministries) in the vision, values, priorities, and strategies necessary to form an apostolically-configured church. We are

---

[2] There's a S.M.A.R.T Way to Write Management's Goals and Objectives, *Management Review* **70** (11): 35-36, 1981.

prioritizing the training of our key leaders in the basics of making disciples.

4) Emphasize character over gifting when selecting leaders.

In selecting ministry leaders, we look for both gifting and character. One cannot carry true spiritual authority without godly character. Our character either enhances or diminishes our capacity to represent the leadership of God. We will avoid the 'plug and play' mentality and not release leaders without preparation and observation.

5) Prepare and distribute a handbook for leaders and members, and develop other resources that reflect the vision, values, and priorities of SCC.

The senior pastor has compiled a handbook explaining our vision, values, priorities, and procedures that has been distributed to all leaders and members. In addition to the handbook, we will develop other resources to communicate our apostolic vision, e.g., books, videos, etc.

6) Preach expository sermons.

The ministry of the Word through expository preaching is an essential way of building spiritual depth into the congregation. These messages are then reviewed in home groups. Focusing on the books of the New Testament strengthens our understanding of the biblical worldview, our identity in Christ, and how to live as citizens in the Kingdom of God.

7) Re-evaluate previous programs and activities.

We will carry out ongoing reviews of the effectiveness and need for previous programs. Often, we spend time, energy, and resources on activities that no longer serve a constructive purpose. We must not be afraid to cull activities or programs when they have outlived their usefulness.

8) Prioritize cells and celebration.

During the initial years of establishing a prototype, we have given priority to activities that strengthen worship services (celebration) and home groups (cells). These are our most visible, shop-front activities that portray who we are.

9) Be prepared to deal with opposition.

To become apostolically-configured means actively pursuing the Spirit-led life. The flesh does not die easily so we need to be prepared for human opposition resulting from immaturity, compromise, the religious spirit, fear, and pride that may surface.

10) Be vigilant in spiritual warfare.

Seeking to establish an apostolically-configured church, makes us a target of spiritual attack. We have an enemy who uses every opportunity to sabotage the work of God, especially when it involves advancing His Kingdom. Prayer and living holy lives deprive Satan of a platform to attack us. We need to keep short accounts with God, be forgiving, not take offense, and be careful of words we speak about others.

The Church at a T-junction

Over the centuries, churches have accumulated beliefs and practices that have little basis in the Scripture, or in the teachings of Jesus and the apostles. The church, in its current state, is not winning the battle against the forces of darkness.

With the Covid-19 pandemic, God has brought churches to a T-junction. At a T-junction, two paths emerge. The first path is business as usual, disengaging with society. The second path is to re-examine our foundations and set a new course.

Church Reformation

When I started out in ministry, I entered a religious system that was influenced by centuries of customs, traditions, and theology. While initially this came as a shock, I learned to conform to what was expected of me as a pastor.

Whenever I raised concerns about the state of the church, denominational leaders would quote a phrase, "*Ecclesia reformata, semper reformanda*" which means "the church reformed, always reforming". This assumes that churches correct themselves as they journey though time, as if set on divine autopilot.

History shows that God's people rarely correct themselves. God had to send His Son to bring correction to the Jewish religious establishment. God sent prophets to ancient Israel to return His people to His ways. God sent reformers to bring correction to the church in the Middle Ages.

Change rarely comes quickly. In my case, the Lord used the ups and downs of ministry over four decades to reveal that I was in an "old wineskin" that needed to change (Matthew 9:17). I needed a wake-up call to see the need for reformation in the church.

Reformation comes through a process of *recognition, realignment,* and *revolution. Recognition* of a problem leads us to *realignment.* We realign by recognizing the priorities and practices of Jesus and the apostles that are relevant and can be put into practice. After *recognition* and *realignment*, we must have courage to take revolutionary action to pursue apostolic alignment.

Reconciliation and Restoration

Reconciliation lies at the heart of God summing up all things in Christ (Ephesians 1:10). Reconciliation takes place at three levels: 1) the Lord has reconciled our individual life to Him when we are born again through faith in Jesus, 2) the reconciliation within the family of believers. This brings forgiveness between believers and unity between churches. 3) Finally, there is the reconciliation of God with His creation, the global perspective of reconciling the earth and every sphere of society back to God's original purposes.

2 Corinthians 5:17-19, "Therefore, if anyone is in Christ, he is a new creation; the old has gone, the new has come! All this is from God, who reconciled us to himself through Christ and gave us the ministry of reconciliation; that God was reconciling the world to himself in Christ, not counting men's sins against them. And he has committed to us the message of reconciliation."

Recently, I felt the time was right to restore my former colleague, Ron Ings and his wife Greta, back into the fellowship of the church. After over ten years of estrangement, the time was right to forgive and be reconciled. Knowing I would face opposition from some, I invited Ron and Greta to stand before the congregation and say whatever they thought needed to be said.

Their words revealed the fruit of repentance, humility, and brokenness. Their courage and honesty deeply touched all who were present. As they spoke, God's power was released to heal broken hearts and set captives free. I was touched when I saw many people in our church go forward to embrace Ron and Greta. In this one powerful act, the Lord revealed the immense power of forgiveness and reconciliation.

Restoration is a process, not a one-time event. In the case of Ron and Greta, there was no attempt to justify their actions. They openly confessed, repented of their sin, and asked forgiveness. The aim of restoration is reconciliation and repentance, and to stop sin from recurring.

The Father's Heart

In the Kingdom, mercy always triumphs over judgement. Henry Wadsworth Longfellow once wrote, "If we could read the secret history of our enemies, we would find in each man's life sorrow and suffering enough to disarm all hostility." In the past, I was often quick to speak and quick to judge. Now, I ask God to show me the hearts of others and how I can respond to them with the Father's heart. Love is the currency of the Kingdom of God. We must learn to spend it generously.

Someday, when we stand before the Lord on the Day of Judgment, I believe He will ask us one important question, *In the course of your life, did you learn how to love?* Our answer to this question will determine our future in eternity. We love in many ways: by persevering instead of giving up, forgiving instead of holding grudges, and doing little acts of kindness that no one will ever see—except God.

One Final Thing

The Kingdom is the highest form of a move from God. It is the revolution the world needs. It is greater than refreshment, greater than revival, and greater than reformation. Why? Refreshment, revival, and reformation are means to an end. They are passing and finite. They all point to establishing the Kingdom of God. The Kingdom is God's goal for creation, the treasure hidden in the field.

Now that you have read my story, you know some of my joys and sorrows. Benjamin Franklin once said, "He who does many things makes many mistakes, but he never makes the greatest mistake of all: doing nothing."

As you can now see, I have done many things in life. I have made some wise decisions and some not so wise. I have discovered on my journey that every experience teaches us something of great value. Every problem is an opportunity in disguise if we learn from our mistakes and do not give up.

One of my favorite Old Testament scriptures is Genesis 50:20. Here, Joseph, now the Prime Minister of Egypt, stands before his brothers, who had earlier sold him into slavery. The brothers, afraid Joseph might seek revenge on them, instead heard these words, "You intended to harm me, but God intended it for good to accomplish what is now being done, the saving of many lives."

A prophet from New Zealand once prophesied over me, "John, God is changing your name to John-Joseph. Like Joseph, you will carry the dreams of many people in your heart." It has taken years, but I can now see how my life has paralleled Joseph's in many ways.

Like Joseph, God has crucified my pride and fleshly attitudes. As for carrying the dreams of others in my heart, you can be the judge of that. My hope is simply to see God's people, the church, become the light of the world, and the salt of the earth. If you share that dream, then this book has accomplished its purpose.

From my balcony overlooking the Indian Ocean, I watch the sun slowly sink to where the sea and sky come together. As the sun disappears beneath the horizon, I pause and thank God for the amazing journey He has taken me on. While it is not what I had expected, it is everything I had hoped for. I thank the Lord for His amazing kindness to me. I have come a long way since watching the California Zephyr disappear into the sunset. I have lived life to the fullest and wouldn't change a thing!

Questions to Consider as Your Way Ahead

---

1. Has the Lord given you a vision or a promise, what is your God-given assignment?

2. How active have you been in pursuing that vison?

3. Do you have spiritual parents? Do you have spiritual children?

4. Do you feel the Lord has called you to truly become involved in the church you attend?

5. Do you resonate with the vision of your church?

6. What are you doing to support the vision?

7. To what extent are your daily activities aligned to your personal and church's vision?

8. Is the Lord king over your life—your spirit, soul, and body?

9. What is your sphere of influence and what are you doing to bring the Kingdom of God into your sphere of influence?

10. How is reconciliation being lived out in your lifestyle?

EXTRA MATERIAL

Southern Cross Association of Churches' Brochure

https://www.southerncrossnetwork.org.au/brochure

Southern Cross Centre Members' Handbook

https://www.southerncrosscentre.org.au/handbook

Southern Cross Association of Churches Online Store

https://www.southerncrossnetwork.org.au/store/

CPSIA information can be obtained
at www.ICGtesting.com
Printed in the USA
BVHW051936030821
613543BV00006B/244